CRAGSIDE

Northumberland

THE NATIONAL TRUST

The National Trust acknowledges with gratitude a great many gifts towards the restoration of Cragside, both of money and in kind. Notable among these are gifts of money from the late Lord Armstrong, Vickers Defence Systems (which has also loaned the portrait of the young Lord Armstrong) and the Ironmongers' Company (for the steel footbridge), and in kind, suites of furniture, sets of china and a marble bust of Sir William Armstrong by Alexander Munro. In addition, generous loans of pictures and pottery by the de Morgan Foundation and of furniture by the Victoria & Albert Museum have been of inestimable value in the work of restoring the house to its former magnificence.

This new guidebook is a much expanded version of that produced by Andrew Saint and Sheila Pettit, when the house first opened in 1979. Chapters One and Two have been written by Mr Saint; Chapter Three by Dr Geoffrey Irlam; and Chapter Four by Prof. Dianne Sachko Macleod. The National Trust is most grateful to them all for their help. Chapter Five has been revised by the National Trust's Historic Buildings Representative for Northumbria, Hugh Dixon, who has also written Chapter Six.

Photographs: Joanna Barnes/James Austin page 68; Bridgeman Art Library/Guildhall Art Gallery page 10; Haslam & Whiteway page 18; National Museum of Wales, Cardiff page 39; National Trust pages 17, 22, 24, 26, 27, 31 (bottom), 32, 75; National Trust Photographic Library page 8; NTPL/Andreas von Einsiedel pages 1, 5, 12, 19, 31 (top), 33, 49, 50, 51, 52, 53, 56, 57, 58, 59, 60, 61, 64, 66, 70; NTPL/Jerry Harpur pages 71, 73; NTPL/Martin Trelawney page 11; NTPL/Rupert Truman pages 4, 44, 45, 76, 77; NTPL/Charlie Waite front cover, pages 37, 62, back cover; NTPL/Derrick E. Witty pages 7 (left and right), 9, 14, 15, 21, 35, 55, 70 (Trustees of the de Morgan Foundation); Newcastle Central Library page 72; Royal Commission on the Historical Monuments of England pages 40, 41; Sotheby's page 38; Turners Photography Ltd pages 16, 20; Carl Eagle/Tyne Photo page 65; Vickers Defence Systems page 6; Newcastle City Library page 23.

CONTENTS

INTRODUCTION

Cragside is the creation of the 1st Lord Armstrong (1810–1900), innovator, engineer and gunmaker. In it are summed up the distinguishing characteristics of one of Britain's greatest scientific geniuses and mightiest industrialists: power, vigour, boldness, romance, sentiment and originality.

The house began as a comparatively small one. It was built between 1863 and 1866 for Sir William Armstrong (as he then was), as a weekend retreat from the cares of his armaments and engineering business at Elswick, just outside Newcastle. It was set in the rugged countryside round Rothbury in Coquetdale which he had known since childhood, on the nucleus of an estate that he was to expand to over 1,700 acres of wooded pleasure grounds and lakes.

The architect of the original house is unknown, but in 1869 Armstrong called in Norman Shaw to transform Cragside into a proper country mansion. By means of his gradual additions over the following fifteen years, the house came to assume its wild, picturesque outline. To Shaw also are due the grandest of Cragside's interiors, which contain some of his best-preserved and most original work. Yet the whole of the building, landscaping and planting were directly in Armstrong's hands. He also brought his scientific and technological expertise to bear upon his home. Cragside was the earliest house in the world to be lit by electricity derived from water power: arc lights were installed in 1878, followed by a much more extensive scheme in 1880 using Joseph Swan's newly invented incandescent lamps. Other examples of Armstrong's ingenuity in the field of hydraulics and engineering are scattered about the house and grounds – justifying a contem-

porary description of Cragside as 'the palace of a modern magician'. Part of his collection of paintings and natural history specimens also remains in the house.

In the end, Cragside is not a house to analyse but to wonder at and enjoy. A unique fusion of art, science and nature, it symbolises not just Lord Armstrong's temperament and career, but also the greatest achievements and contrasts of the Victorian age.

(Left) The entrance front
(Right) The Dining Room table set for dessert

CHAPTER ONE
LORD ARMSTRONG AND HIS FIRM

The creator of Cragside, William George Armstrong, was born on 26 November 1810 at 9 Pleasant Row, Shieldfield, Newcastle upon Tyne. He was the second child and only son of William Armstrong (1778–1857), a Newcastle corn merchant. His mother, Anne, was the daughter of William Potter, who owned a colliery in the village of Walbottle, a few miles west of Newcastle.[1]

The circumstances of Armstrong's childhood were easy. The Potters were well established locally, and Anne Armstrong is reputed to have been a woman of some culture. His father, however, had made his own way into Tyneside mercantile society. He had come to Newcastle in the 1790s from modest origins in Wreay near Carlisle, found

William Armstrong; by James Ramsay, 1831 (Study). Painted while Armstrong was still a law student

work as a clerk with a firm of corn merchants on the quayside, and in due course became owner of the business. William Armstrong the elder was a man of broad attainments. He was an early member of the Newcastle Literary and Philosophical Society and a keen mathematician and natural historian. These accomplishments he passed on in full measure to his son. In 1835, the year of the great reform of English town government, he ventured into Newcastle politics, taking a shrewd interest in the management of the River Tyne – something critical to the city's prosperity. In 1850 this 'zealous, active and industrious merchant'[2] crowned his career by becoming Newcastle's mayor. Addison Potter, his brother-in-law, had been mayor five years before.

The young William, a delicate boy, went to schools in and close to Newcastle, followed at the age of 16 by a spell of two years at a grammar school in Bishop Auckland. There he met the Ramshaw family, Bishop Auckland builders and engineers, and developed his juvenile talent for mechanics. But his father had other ideas. He wanted his son to follow the law and join the firm of Armorer Donkin, the prosperous Newcastle solicitor who was the family's closest friend. A bachelor who looked upon William as an adoptive son, and an amateur scientist himself, Donkin was to be a great influence on the young man's career. He lived in suburban Jesmond and had a country retreat at Rothbury – exactly the places where Armstrong himself was to make his homes. In 1828 Armstrong took articles under Donkin. He then quickly went to London to gain a high-class legal training under the tutelage of his brother-in-law, William Henry Watson (1796–1860), a Special Pleader at Lincoln's Inn. It was in this year that his only sister, Anne, Watson's wife, died at the early age of 26, leaving a small boy, John William Watson (1827–1909), who was to be the father of Armstrong's eventual heir.

Armorer Donkin; by an unknown artist (Gallery). Donkin was a Newcastle solicitor who befriended the young Armstrong and encouraged him to pursue a scientific career

Armstrong spent five years in London before returning to Newcastle. There, in 1833, he was admitted into the law partnership of Donkin, Stable and Armstrong. But his benevolent mentor, Armorer Donkin, gave him scope to pursue his mechanical and scientific bent. 'All the time,' recollected Armstrong later, 'although I had no idea of abandoning the law and regularly attended to my professional duties, I was an amateur scientist, constantly experimenting and studying in my leisure time.'[3] He soon proposed marriage to Margaret Ramshaw (1807–93), daughter of the Bishop Auckland builder he had got to know while at school. They were married in 1835 and set up house together at Jesmond, in a newly-built house known as Jesmond Dene (long since demolished).

Not much is known of the future Lady Armstrong. A little older than her husband, she seems perfectly to have fulfilled the ideal of kind, sup-

portive but withdrawn Victorian helpmeet. The couple's childlessness only serves to increase her obscurity. She was, however, said to have been a keen botanist, and played a big part in the planting of the grounds at both Jesmond Dene and Cragside.[4]

The year 1835 also marks the time from which Armstrong's experiments took on a palpably practical direction. They coincided with the surge in confidence, energy and wealth that overtook Tyneside in the post-1815 phase of the Industrial Revolution. Water, coal, iron, steam, the first railways and the navigability of the Tyne were the key factors in this 'quantum leap'. Behind them all

Margaret Ramshaw married Armstrong in 1835 and helped to lay out the gardens at both Jesmond Dene and Cragside; watercolour by H. H. Emmerson from the album presented to the Armstrongs following the royal visit in 1884 (Watercolour Gallery)

'Iron and Coal'; by William Bell Scott (Wallington). William Armstrong played a leading role in the rapid industrialisation of Tyneside in the nineteenth century

lay the quest for efficient power. During that heroic era of Newcastle's industrial advancement, the sense of common civic interest and progress was keen. Firms were small and family-owned, transactions national in scope at most, and labour disputes negligible. Enlightened merchants, colliery- and ship-owners, builders, engineers, lawyers and civic figures met within the confines of the Newcastle 'Lit and Phil' to thrash out their problems and promote technical and commercial advances. With his mechanical genius, legal training, local patriotism and family connections, Armstrong fitted this milieu to perfection.

Water – still for most of the nineteenth century the prime source of power for Britain's industries – was Armstrong's first and favourite field of endeavour, and the fount of his later fortune. It was while fishing (his greatest hobby) in Yorkshire in the year of his marriage that the inefficiency of an overshot waterwheel set him thinking about the potential for power that lay untapped within a column of water. From then on, to quote a family saying, 'William had water on the brain'.[5] Hydraulics became his passion. Great improvements in applied hydraulics for driving machinery had already been made by a century of English engineers and millwrights. Armstrong felt sure that more could be done. He made his first attempt in 1838–9, during the building of Robert Stephenson's High Level Bridge at Newcastle. Together with Henry Watson, the contractor for the bridge, he designed and made a new rotatory hydraulic engine run from the town's main water supply. But the water pressure was too weak. The machine produced only 5 horsepower, and no one took it up.

In 1840 Armstrong was sidetracked by the experience of a Cramlington colliery engineer into examining the phenomenon of electricity generated by effluent steam – what is now known as the 'Armstrong Effect' (see Chapter Three). He wrote papers on the subject, corresponded with Michael Faraday, the doyen of British electrical studies, and had a series of hydro-electric machines made which could generate dramatic sparks. With these he gave popular lectures in Newcastle and London. They

had no immediate upshot. But the investigation of the Armstrong Effect had lasting scientific value. In recognition, Armstrong was elected a Fellow of the Royal Society while still a practising solicitor. Thereafter water and the generation of electricity were linked in his mind – a link which came to fruition nearly forty years later at Cragside.

So far Armstrong had 'swung like an erratic pendulum between the law office and the lathe'.[6] The first of the steps which transformed him into a full-time manufacturer was his promotion of the Whittle Dene Water Company in 1844–5. This company aimed to replace the city's much-criticised water supply with a more powerful and scientific system fed from reservoirs at Whittle Dene 10 miles west of the city. It was masterminded by Armstrong as its secretary and supported by the best Newcastle businessmen of the day, including his uncle, Addison Potter. The scheme was a complete and rapid success. But Armstrong himself was less concerned with the general issues of water supply than with using the higher pressure now obtainable to power machinery – specifically the cranes of Newcastle's docks, on whose efficiency the city's welfare so much depended. Early in 1846, one of the quayside cranes was experimentally converted by means of a combined hydraulic ram and pulley device. It proved so successful that four others were soon built by Henry Watson. This initiative was undertaken

The Elswick works; by Thomas M. Hemy. From 1847 Armstrong transformed this area of the upper Tyne into the heart of his industrial empire

The opening of Tower Bridge in 1894; by W. L. Wyllie (Guildhall Art Gallery). W. G. Armstrong & Company supplied the hydraulic lifting gear for Tower Bridge

by the Newcastle Cranage Company, effectively a subsidiary of the Whittle Dene company.

In order properly to promote his various machines, patents and enterprises, the next logical step for Armstrong was to abandon the law and go into manufacturing. W. G. Armstrong & Company – a private partnership between Armstrong, Armorer Donkin, Addison Potter, George Cruddas and Richard Lambert – was created at the beginning of 1847. Elswick, the district on the upper reaches of the Tyne envisaged by the great Newcastle builder Richard Grainger as a new industrial suburb for the city, became the natural location for the company's works. The first buildings were soon erected and production commenced in the autumn of 1847. All manner of equipment and machines were made in the first years: lathes, pumps, winding engines, dock gates, steam engines, several bridges and even an experimental condensing locomotive. But the staple of the early firm was the Armstrong hydraulic crane. According to tradition the first order,

for the Albert Docks at Liverpool, came as a result of the dexterous antics of a docker called 'Hydraulic Jack' with Newcastle Quayside's No. 1 Crane in front of an astonished Jesse Hartley, the engineer to Liverpool docks. The order book soon expanded to the point where an average of two cranes per week were being made.

The secret of the company's early growth was Armstrong's ability to keep innovating. Perhaps his greatest invention and, in the words of his biographer, Peter McKenzie, 'the key to the general adoption of hydraulic systems'[7] came in 1850-1, when he introduced the hydraulic accumulator, a means of increasing water pressure by subjecting a static column of water to a great weight, raised by a pumping engine. This obviated the need for an old-fashioned high water tower or great natural fall of water for hydraulic systems. Greatly increased pressures now became possible, soon reaching over a thousand pounds per square inch.

The first Armstrong cranes worked from an accumulator were at New Holland on the Humber, one of several early projects upon which Armstrong worked closely with the prolific dock and bridge engineer James Meadows Rendel. In gratitude for

Rendel's encouragement, Armstrong befriended and supported the engineer's three younger sons after their father's sudden death in 1856 and took them all into his firm.[8] George Wightwick Rendel became a partner in 1858 and was for many years a fertile engineering designer in the armaments and shipbuilding side of the business; eventually in the 1880s he was to direct the Italian subsidiary, the Armstrong-Pozzuoli Company near Naples. Stuart Rendel, like Armstrong a lawyer by training, ran the London office for many years before going into Liberal politics and being raised to the peerage. The youngest son, Hamilton Rendel, spent his whole career as an engineering designer with Armstrongs. The paternal loyalty shown to the Rendel boys by the childless Armstrong no doubt reflected the support he himself received from Armorer Donkin. In the same way he took Henry Brunel, son of Isambard Kingdom Brunel, under his wing after the great railway engineer's premature death in 1859. Henry Brunel too remained with Armstrongs for years. The sublime and sensuous engines that once powered the bascules of London's Tower Bridge, opened in 1894, were designed and installed by Hamilton Rendel and Henry Brunel working together. They are today the best-preserved and most accessible example of the Armstrong company's moving machinery.

Gunmaking, too, with which the Armstrong name and firm has become for better or worse identified, started with the Rendel connection. In November 1854 J. M. Rendel and Armstrong had a discussion about the ponderous, outdated nature of heavy ordnance, whose limitations were then being savagely exposed in the Crimean War. Rendel pressed his friend to develop and put to the Government his ideas for light, breech-loading guns firing elongated projectiles rather than the old-fashioned cannonballs, and with the barrels made of wrought-iron sheets shrunk upon a rifled steel core. None of these ideas was new, but for years there had been no radically fresh initiative in ordnance manufacture, and no one had yet solved the metallurgical problems involved. The Crimean fiasco forced the Government to rethink arms production and supply, and to back innovation. Armstrong's timing was perfect.

After a long period of trials, prototypes and committees – in which Armstrong's legal experience proved invaluable – his gun was in November 1858 pronounced more reliable and accurate than the designs of his rivals, notably the Manchester industrialist Joseph Whitworth. In return for giving up his patents to the Government, he received a knighthood and was appointed Chief Engineer of Rifled Ordnance to the War Department and (a little later) Superintendent of the Royal Gun Factory at Woolwich. At first, only Elswick was in a position to make the Armstrong gun. To do so the Elswick Ordnance Works was founded, run by a separate company under the direction of Captain Andrew Noble, a young gunnery expert whom Armstrong had met in the course of the ordnance trials. Noble was to be Armstrong's right-hand man of business for the rest of his life.

The years 1859–63 were the acme of Armstrong's career. During this period Elswick acted as a monopoly supplier of heavy arms to the British Government and continued to stride ahead in civil production. Armstrong himself toiled unceasingly. His government commitments obliged him to open a London office at 8 Great George Street, in the

Armstrong guns defended the Needles Old Battery on the Isle of Wight

heart of the engineering district of Westminster, which he shared with Alexander Rendel, J.M.Rendel's oldest son and successor, and where he stayed in a flat as need required. He was chairman of the Whittle Dene Water Company throughout these years and President of the Institution of Mechanical Engineers in 1861–2. He was also much involved with the British Association for the Advancement of Science. At the Association's annual meeting in 1863, held in Newcastle under his presidency, he gave a masterly address about energy resources in the North East of England. Despite all this, Armstrong kept up a punishing programme of technological research.

In 1862, under political pressure following criticism of the performance of Armstrong guns in the third China War, the Government announced that it would drop all its gunnery contracts with Elswick. This marked a turning point in Armstrong's life and that of his firm. He resigned his

government appointments and amalgamated the ordnance and engineering firms. If the armaments side was not to close, the company's only recourse was the hitherto untried one of seeking foreign orders. The American Civil War was then raging, and the company soon had spectacular successes with sales to both sides. This shift of emphasis was prophetic of changes throughout Victorian industry and society. A brilliantly successful civil engineering firm with a sideline in guns was on the brink of transformation into a symbol of imperial might. While Armstrong presided over this new direction and dutifully entertained princes and envoys who were to flock to Newcastle to order arms (at first in a specially built banqueting hall in Jesmond Dene, later at Cragside), the burgeoning foreign arms trade was of little personal interest to him.

By degrees he became less concerned in the day-to-day running of his firm, and transferred his energies to other projects like the building of

Armstrong probably acquired the onyx surround for the Library fireplace during his trip to Egypt in 1872

Cragside, begun in 1863. The process of separation was slow. When in 1868 the company expanded into building warships in partnership with the firm of Charles Mitchell, further down the Tyne at Walker, Armstrong was still very much in charge. But a watershed came in 1871 when skilled engineering workers struck nationally for a nine-hour day. Armstrong, the head of the Newcastle engineering employers' association, took an intransigent line, blundered in negotiation, and was humiliated. The early Victorian paternalism in industrial relations which he believed in – he had built a school and an institute at Elswick – was becoming out of date. Soon after this experience Armstrong went on his one known long holiday abroad, to Egypt. On his return he gave vivid lectures to the Newcastle 'Lit and Phil' on his observations and experiences, later collected into a book.[9] His visit had included a voyage up the Nile to see the cataracts and a trip to the pyramids, the construction of which fascinated him.

In the 1870s Armstrong withdrew increasingly to country life and an honorific role in his company. The change was finally confirmed in 1882, when the Armstrong and Mitchell firms joined force as a new public company, Sir W. G. Armstrong, Mitchell & Company. Two million pounds were subscribed, and a grand expansion took place under Sir Andrew Noble, chiefly to boost the production of armaments and ironclads. Steel-making too was added to the firm's capabilities. The last 15 years of the century marked the high point of the Armstrong firm's formidable international reputation. Over half the Japanese ironclads employed in their victorious naval war against Russia in 1905, for instance, were made by Armstrongs. Its only rivals were Krupps of Essen, and Krupps, unlike Armstrongs, was directly subsidised by their government. A final, symbolic take-over was that of the old rivals, Whitworths, in 1897. By the time of Armstrong's death in 1900, the company employed some 25,000 workers on 300 acres at Elswick and nearby. But successful innovation became rarer in the later years of Noble's regime. Sir W.G.Armstrong, Whitworth & Company was subsequently taken over in turn by the more dynamic and flexible firm of Vickers of Sheffield.

In his later years, Armstrong turned his talents in two directions. He used his technological genius for private ends and study, while his administrative and legal capacities were devoted to making wise public use of the vast fortune he had acquired. At Cragside, he created the most extensive and ingenious hydraulic system ever found on a country estate, one that pumped water, turned spits, powered a sawmill, farm machinery and a dairy, made silage and, eventually, ran a dynamo providing electric light. Electric lighting became practicable only in the 1870s, first in the form of harsh arc lights, then in the kinder guise of the incandescent filament bulbs invented almost simultaneously by Edison and by Armstrong's friend Joseph Swan. Such were Armstrong's love of electricity and alertness to innovation that he was the first person known to have experimented with domestic arc lighting and the first to have a permanent domestic installation of filament lamps. Over the years he expanded and altered the Cragside generating and lighting system many times. While in his eighties he also renewed his personal experiments with electricity, investigating both high-tension current and the nature of electrical discharges. The results of Armstrong's experiments with discharges were issued as a folio book, *Electric Movement in Air and Water*, published in 1897 with beautiful photographs by his friend John Worsnop of Rothbury.

Armstrong inherited from his father a sense of public duty. Though basically indifferent to party politics, he felt strongly enough against Irish Home Rule to stand for Parliament in Newcastle as a Liberal Unionist in 1886. He was defeated, not to his great regret: 'It is dangerous to meddle with public affairs if one wishes for peace and quietness as I do', he told George Rendel a few years later.[10] But in 1887 he was created the 1st Baron Armstrong of Cragside and spoke on a few occasions in the House of Lords. Between 1889 and 1892 he also sat on the Northumberland County Council.

Much of his immense wealth was devoted to benefactions in favour of Newcastle. In 1878 he gave what is now the Armstrong Park to the City Corporation, adding the rest of Jesmond Dene in 1884. He made many gifts to the Royal Victoria Infirmary, which was rebuilt following a donation in his memory by his heir William Watson-Armstrong in 1901. He and his wife gave large sums to Newcastle's Hancock Museum of Natural History, and endowed the College of Physical Science – originally part of Durham University, later Armstrong College within Newcastle University. This last gift is perhaps a surprise, since Armstrong was a paternalist on matters of industrial training, believing that a selective, high-class apprenticeship system like the one in operation at Elswick was sufficient, and denouncing what he once called 'the vague cry for technical education'. The one great Armstrong benefaction that failed to materialise was at Bamburgh Castle, which he purchased in 1894 after his wife's death, intending to convert it into a convalescent home in her memory. A scheme of conversion – not, it must be said, architectually distinguished – was begun under the direction of the architect C. J. Ferguson of Carlisle, but was left unfinished at the time of his death. In due course Bamburgh became the second seat of the Armstrongs.

'The most significant feature of Armstrong's

William Armstrong in old age; by Mary Lemon Waller, 1898 (No. 15; Library)

character', writes Peter McKenzie, 'is its absolute normality.'[11] Genius and breadth of achievement such as his invite the envious idea that there must have been something strange or lopsided about the man. There is nothing to support this, nor can one detect a hint of the hidden personal aggressiveness that some might want to seek in the psyche of a great armaments manufacturer. Armstrong was unfailingly portrayed by his contemporaries as assured, balanced, kind, considerate, lucid in speech and writing, loyal and easy towards his manifold friends, a good judge of men and a wise delegator, untouched by snobbery, affectionate towards children, and modest in personal appearance and speech. The only eccentricity that can be detected is a 'peculiar shuffling side gait',[12] and this was probably a trait of old age. Doubtless it was his essential calmness of character that allowed Armstrong to achieve so much both in science and in business, and then to switch almost effortlessly from these pursuits to a simpler, more rustic but no less energetic style of life in his later years. It is perhaps the very undramatic nature of Armstrong's character, its apparent lack of mania or obsession, which prevent him being better acknowledged as one of the greatest of Victorian Englishmen.

NOTES

1 David Dougan, *The Great Gunmaker*, 1970, pp. 20–5; Peter McKenzie, *W. G. Armstrong*, 1983, pp. 10–11; *Dictionary of Business Biography*, i, 1984, pp. 68–74.

2 Dougan, op. cit., p. 27.

3 Ibid., p. 27.

4 *Newcastle Daily Journal*, 4 September 1893.

5 *The Northern Counties Magazine*, 1, 1900–1, p. 326.

6 *The Monthly Chronicle of North Country Lore and Legend*, January 1889, p. 2.

7 McKenzie, op. cit., p. 47. See also Ian McNeil, *Hydraulic Power*, 1972, pp. 58–77.

8 Michael R. Lane, *The Rendel Connection*, 1989, pp. 48–9, 64–73.

9 Sir W. G. Armstrong, *A Visit to Egypt*, 1872.

10 McKenzie, op. cit., p. 113.

11 Ibid., p. 123.

12 Id.

CHAPTER TWO

THE BUILDING OF CRAGSIDE

'I believe I first came here as a baby in arms,' reminisced Lord Armstrong in 1888 about Rothbury, 'and my earliest recollections consist of paddling in the Coquet, gathering pebbles on its gravel beds, and climbing amongst the rocks on the Crag.'[1] During his childhood in the 1810s and '20s, his parents used to come at least once a year from Newcastle to stay with their friends, the Donkins, who had a house at Rothbury. William was a delicate boy, with a bad chest. 'More than once,' he remembered, 'an apparently incurable cough was quickly removed by coming to Rothbury, and had it not been for its curative effect there would have been no Cragside at this day.'[2] Over the years he explored Upper Coquetdale, learned to fish expertly, and grew to know and love the secluded glen through which the Debdon Burn forces its way to the Coquet.

Returning to Rothbury and fishing in the Coquet remained a favourite pastime of Armstrong's during his early married life. 'I have been almost continuously in the water this glorious day', he wrote to his wife from Rothbury in May 1843, 'and there is nothing does me so much good.'[3] But from 1847, when Armstrong set up his great engineering company, he had no time for holidays. For years at a stretch he worked at fever pitch. The hardest period of all was 1859–63, when Armstrong combined the intensive applied scientific research, which was his first love, with managing the Elswick works and two exacting posts in London, advising the Government on the design and manufacture of artillery.

The year 1863 was a watershed. The Government had begun to rely less on Armstrong's help, and ceased for years to place any new orders for ordnance with the Elswick works. Tired, disappointed but ever resilient, Armstrong resigned his government appointments and faced the prospect of reorganising the company. Already he was starting to devolve the running of Elswick. That summer Armstrong came back to Rothbury for the first time in 15 years, along with his partners Andrew Noble and George Rendel and their families.[4] He was then fifty-two.

(Right) As a child Armstrong was fond of playing among the burns of Upper Coquetdale. In 1884 the three children of the Prince and Princess of Wales and an unknown girl did the same; watercolour by H. H. Emmerson from the album commemorating the royal visit now displayed in the Watercolour Gallery

On impulse, he decided to buy as much of the Debdon valley as he could. He had no sense then of acquiring a 'country estate' in the conventional sense. The land was poor, mostly too rough for farming and neglected, with just a few dilapidated buildings. Nor was its ownership in a single hand. Armstrong managed to buy an initial tract of 20 acres from Archdeacon Thorp in November 1863. Straightaway he started upon what he termed 'a small house in the neighbourhood for occasional visits in the summer time'.[5] It took its name from Cragend Hill above the house. 'So eager was he that work should proceed as rapidly as possible,' says the local historian D. D. Dixon (speaking perhaps of the following summer of 1864), 'that he and Lady Armstrong, together with Mr and Mrs Bertram [the agent and his wife], took up their abode in the miller's house, which consisted of four rooms only . . . until the new house was sufficiently advanced to permit their moving into it.'[6]

The original Cragside was a modest, two-storey picturesque 'lodge', suitable for small shooting or fishing parties. It was built in rock-faced stone and had fancy bargeboards to the gables, a pantiled roof, an entrance porch at a queer angle, and a water-tower on top. It was not fundamentally an ambitious building and its designer is unknown. A remote possibility is John Dobson, the most famous of Newcastle's Victorian architects. Dobson had added to Armstrong's house at Jesmond Dene and built him a separate banqueting hall there, but he had retired by 1863. Nevertheless Armstrong's property at Jesmond, later to be given by him to the city of Newcastle, became a first model for the new estate. Jesmond Dene had dramatic natural features not unlike those of Cragside, though on a smaller, suburban scale. Armstrong and his wife Margaret had spent much time and energy in landscaping and planting at Jesmond. That first-hand experience was soon in evidence at Cragside. From the first, they took charge of operations themselves. In these early years, 'more attention was devoted to covering the bare hill sides with foliage than to building anything great in the shape of a house.'[7] The lodges, the garden buildings at Knocklaw and a stable block were among the original works. The house itself, 'practically built on its own quarry', at first 'appeared almost lost amongst the huge crags by which it was surrounded.'[8] When it was first lived in we do not know, but given Armstrong's im-

The first house, before Norman Shaw's additions

patience it was probably during 1864, when wall-papers were being ordered from Morris & Co. The homely scale and conventional taste of these first interiors can still be savoured in the Study.

Over and above the formidable work of taming the terrain, Armstrong soon began to experiment with hydraulic technology at Cragside. To avoid repetition of the water shortage which occurred when the Debdon Burn dried up in 1865, he dammed the stream to form Tumbleton Lake the following year. Below it he installed a hydraulic ram which pumped water to the gardens, and also to a reservoir which fed a tank in one of the house's towers. On his first visit to Cragside in 1869, Norman Shaw enthused to his wife about the 'wonderful hydraulic machines that do all sorts of things you can imagine'.[9]

'It will be very satisfactory working for Sir William as he knows right well what he is about', wrote Shaw in the same letter. Encouraged by the projected extension of the Northumberland Central Railway to Rothbury, which promised to make Newcastle accessible in little more than an hour, Armstrong now decided to turn Cragside into his principal home. Though he had big extensions in mind, he can hardly have imagined the size the house was to attain in the fullness of time. But from about 1870 he began systematically to buy adjacent land, not only to add to the grounds of Cragside, but also for farming. Eventually he was to own 1,729 acres surrounding the house as well as large tracts of farmland around Rothbury.

The London architect upon whom Armstrong called to extend Cragside in 1869, Richard Norman

Richard Norman Shaw (seated) with his early business partner, W. Eden Nesfield, c.1873

Shaw (1831–1912), was not then well known. The choice confirms Armstrong as a shrewd judge of talent. Cragside was among the jobs that were to catapult Shaw to the top of his profession as a fresh, brilliant and flexible designer of picturesque houses. The Armstrongs seem to have got to know him through the painter J. C. Horsley, with whom they socialised on their frequent visits to London in the 1860s. Horsley was a brother-in-law of Isambard Kingdom Brunel. Following Brunel's death in 1859, Armstrong had shown kindness to the great engineer's son Henry. Armstrong and his wife were also growing interested in the arts, particularly contemporary painting, examples of which hung in the banqueting hall at Jesmond Dene. Norman Shaw had already worked for Horsley and for another painter friendly with the Armstrongs, the marine artist E. W. Cooke. He had also designed the Brunel Memorial Window in Westminster Abbey. His first task for Armstrong – if a sleek set of dessert knives and forks with agate handles, seemingly made for the Armstrongs in 1868 and attributable to Shaw, is excepted – was a small extension to the Jesmond Dene banqueting hall (1869–70). Its purpose was to accommodate a large canvas by Horsley, *Prince Hal taking the Crown from his Father's Bedside*, which had failed to find a niche in the Palace of Westminster. But in October 1869 Shaw came on to Rothbury for a weekend and was given the grander job of enlarging Cragside.

Shaw's first houses of note had been in the Kent and Sussex Weald, and their architecture was tailored to the ease and sweetness of that region of southern England. He had built extensions to an old farmhouse near Cranbrook for Horsley (1864–5), and a new house, Glen Andred, Groombridge, for Cooke (1866–8). Then, just before Cragside, came a second and bigger house at Groombridge – Leyswood (1868–9). Its publication in 1871 was to cause an architectural sensation. All these buildings were in the pretty, red-brick-and-tile-hung 'Old English' or 'Sussex house' idiom, which had been more or less invented by Shaw and his equally clever early partner, W. E. Nesfield. What Nesfield and Shaw were endeavouring to do was to take the domestic architecture of the Victorian picturesque tradition, so often stiff, angular and bitty, and to

Norman Shaw's first commission from Armstrong was to design a set of dessert knives and forks, which are decorated with the Armstrong initial and the sunflower motif also found on the north front of Cragside

give it spice, suavity, local colour, richness and articulation. Leyswood, built on a boulder-strewn eminence with some similarity to Cragside, was the first house in which these ideas came off on a large scale.

The extensions to Cragside were a challenge to Shaw. He had built almost nothing domestic in the north of England before. He was obliged to temper his new-found southern style to the tough and stony traditions of Northumbrian building. The first Cragside was just the kind of villa he felt he could improve upon: knobbly, bony and fiddly, and just plonked down in the magnificent landscape. Yet in 1869 Armstrong wanted Shaw merely to add to the existing house's north end, not to improve or supplant it. Gradually Shaw gained himself more room for architectural manoeuvre. But in 15 years working at Cragside he was never given the free hand he wanted. It says much for his affability, patience and pliancy that he never seems to have crossed swords with Armstrong, even when the great industrialist's independence of mind and hand-to-mouth approach prevented the creation of the unified architectural masterpiece that Cragside might have become. In the end, Shaw was dispassionate enough to view his great houses less as his own personal creations than as the playthings of those who paid for them. At Cragside that was certainly the case.

According to the story, Shaw sketched out the whole of his scheme for Cragside while the guests were out shooting.[10] If that is true, he can have done little more than indicate the lines of future extensions. The immediate brief was to add a library and dining-room on the north end of the house, with a plunge bath and hot-air heating system in the basement, and two storeys of bedrooms above. Work began on this addition in 1870. The basic work here and on all the extensions that followed was undertaken not by a building contractor but by local masons under the direct supervision of Armstrong's faithful agent, William Bertram.

The fitting-up of the interiors, involving skilled trades and London craftsmen, was still proceeding in 1872. We do not have names, but it is likely that the rich oak and walnut joinery, so superb a feature throughout Shaw's interiors of the 1870s at Cragside, was supplied from London by the firm of W. H. Lascelles. Special items of stone and wood carving were undertaken by James Forsyth, a trusted collaborator of Shaw and Nesfield. The Library and Dining Room survive untampered with. Indeed they are Shaw's only complete early interiors to remain anywhere with their furnishings intact, and they are masterpieces of English interior decoration of the 1870s. The Library is perhaps the subtlest country-house interior of its day. It shows how in his early career Shaw liked to set off the ponderousness of Gothic woodwork with a medley of colourful and luxurious items: stained glass, exotic chairs and fabrics, blue-and-white pots, and naturalistic relief carving. On the outside Shaw's smooth ashlarwork, forcefully bayed windows and cannonading chimneys on the 1870–2 extension are in a different class of attainment from the original rock-faced villa, though later changes on the north side obscure this.

By the time this first extension was completed, Armstrong was ready for further enlargements. There may indeed have been no real intermission in the works. Thus far, the house of 1863 had not been altered on the south or west. Then in April 1872 Shaw exhibited perspective drawings at the Royal Academy showing both these fronts remodelled in smooth masonry and raised, and the central tower topped with a half-timbered gable – hardly a genuine Northumbrian feature. Clearly he wanted to get rid of traces of the original elevations. But Armstrong had other priorities. He was happy to add bedrooms over the former house, heighten the tower and build a new entrance. But he could not be bothered to reface the old glen front.

Instead, by early 1873 at the latest Armstrong had decided to build a long new wing to the east of the entrance. This was to contain his 'museum' and observatory, and to end with what was to be called

Shaw's decoration of the Dining Room has survived remarkably unaltered. The light oak dado was carved with birds and flowers by James Forsyth

South West prospect of Cragside, Northumberland

Shaw's perspective drawing of proposed changes to the west front, 1872

the Gilnockie Tower in honour of the sixteenth-century John Armstrong of Gilnockie, 'that moss-trooper so famous in border song'[11] and a supposed ancestor of Sir William. So Shaw designed a new and long south entrance front, with two further timber gables on the left over a new front door, a roof dipping down low over the museum or gallery, and then a handsome high gable atop the Gilnockie Tower. For the time being, however, Armstrong opted to finish off the tower with an observatory dome instead of a gable, so giving that end of the front a stunted look. These works were proceeding throughout 1873. In November of that year Shaw designed Cragside's third and last tower, the northern gateway at the back of the house with a connecting corridor at ground level to the west.

All these extensions seem to have been finished by the end of 1874. At this point the house was all but complete in outline, with the significant exception of the south-east wing containing the Drawing Room and Billiard Room.

From about 1875 Armstrong was living for most of the year at Cragside. But his restless mind was continually bent on improvements. A large payment to Shaw in 1877 may reflect internal changes, perhaps the remodelling of the staircase or the fitting-out of the 'owl bedrooms'. These were also the years in which Armstrong added most to his picture collections. By the end of 1878, he had turned his museum into a picture gallery and was lighting it with a turbine-powered arc lamp – one of

(Right) The Prince of Wales at Cragside in 1884. Armstrong is sitting opposite (in top hat); watercolour by H. H. Emmerson (Watercolour Gallery)

the earliest experiments of its kind. In December 1880 the electric lighting within the house was elaborated, using the new and kinder incandescent carbon-filament lamps invented in the previous year by Armstrong's friend Joseph Swan of Newcastle. Altogether 45 of these lamps were installed by Swan and Armstrong in the house, though they were never all used at once. Later, the equipment was several times modified and extended. After 1886 the current came from a new hydroelectric power house built at Burnfoot rather than from the engine house below Debdon Lake (see Chapter Three). Armstrong was proud of the simplicity and economy of the whole scheme. 'The brook, in fact, lights the house,' he wrote in 1881, 'and there is no consumption of any material in the process.'[12]

For as long as the Armstrongs retained their grounds and banqueting hall at Jesmond Dene on the outskirts of Newcastle, they had no need of a grand suite of reception rooms at Cragside in which to entertain the foreign dignitaries who were increasingly the Armstrong firm's customers for guns and ironclads. But in the early 1880s he decided to give the Jesmond Dene park to the City of Newcastle and to dispense hospitality at Cragside instead (though he kept his house in Jesmond). By May 1883 Shaw had begun work on designing his final contribution to Cragside: the south-east or Drawing Room wing, modelled externally on Haddon Hall in Derbyshire, but with a large top-lit interior space and sumptuous chimney-piece indicative of the growing formality of his architecture. The wing was complete by August 1884, when the Prince and Princess of Wales came to stay while on a tour of the North East. To mark the event, the town of Rothbury presented Armstrong with a book of watercolours illustrating the visit, painted by the Northumbrian artists J. T. Dixon and H. H. Emmerson. (It is now displayed in the Watercolour Gallery.) Other stately entourages were accommodated over the succeeding years. The King of Siam, the Shah of Persia (1889) and the Crown Prince of Afghanistan (1895) were among the potentates who came to Cragside for the sake of arms deals.

The visit of the Prince and Princess of Wales marked the culmination of a 20-year process which had transformed the quaint little villa on the crag into an embodiment of northern romance, artistry, power and wealth – the bourgeois, British equivalent of such mighty fastnesses as Ludwig II's Neuschwanstein in Bavaria, or Kaiser Wilhelm's Haut Koenigsbourg in Alsace:

Ten thousand small glass lamps were hung amongst the rocky hillsides or upon the lines of railing which guard the walks, and an almost equal number of Chinese lanterns were swung across leafy glades, and continued pendant from tree to tree in sinuous lines, miles in extent. For the lighting of all this enormous illumination alone a large staff of men was required, and those employed started on their lengthy and difficult tasks almost as soon as the Royal guests had sought their apartments in Cragside. For nearly two hours the task was proceeded with, and at the end of that time darkness had fallen over the outer landscape ... The château itself was a blaze of light. From every window the bright rays of the electric lamps shone with purest radiance, and the main front was made brilliant by a general illumination. A magnificent pyrotechnic display, under the management of Mr. James Pain, of London, took place on Rothbury Hill. An immense bonfire was also lit on the top of Simonside Hill.[3]

Many alterations were made to Cragside after 1884. But the details we know about them are frustratingly few. Norman Shaw was not employed by Armstrong after this date, though in about 1887 (the year in which Armstrong became a peer) the observatory dome was removed and the Gilnockie Tower completed according to Shaw's original design. Some of the many decorative changes to the minor rooms were perhaps made at the behest of Armstrong's great-nephew, William Henry Watson-Armstrong (1863–1941), grandson of his short-lived sister Anne and son of John and Margaret Watson of Adderstone Hall, Belford. As William Henry Watson, he had come to live at Cragside and to act as manager for his great-uncle's estates in the late 1880s. On marrying Winifreda Adye in 1889 he was formally adopted as Armstrong's heir, and changed his name to Watson-Armstrong. From then on the young couple spent much of the year at Cragside. It was in 1889 that the Gallery seems to have taken on its present form, the original open steel stanchions being cased in with woodwork, the front windows blocked, and the roof awkwardly raised to accommodate top-lighting for the pictures. For some time Armstrong had had a small laboratory set into the hill behind the Drawing Room. In 1895, aged nearly 85 and two years a widower, he commissioned a new Billiard Room and electrical room in this position from the architect Frederick W. Waller of Gloucester (the Waller family was for many years friendly with the Armstrongs). These were designed in a respectable Tudor-Jacobean style in reasonable keeping with the Drawing Room.

Some of the buildings in the inner courtyard and the north front probably also date from the 1890s. Armstrong's vigour was by no means impaired at this time. Versed as he now was in the Cragside style, it is possible that he designed some of these extensions himself, for some of them are curiously coarse and seem to betray an engineer's hand rather than that of an architect. A possible candidate for their design is C. J. Ferguson of Carlisle, the architect employed on the conversion of Bamburgh Castle, which Armstrong purchased in 1893. In 1892–3 Armstrong extended the home farm and stables by Tumbleton Lake. Here a trained architect was more certainly involved, but again we do not know whom.

Lord Armstrong died at Cragside on 27 December 1900, leaving the sum of £1,400,000 gross. As he and his wife had no children, the title then lapsed. Their estates and interests, including over 10,000 acres of land in Northumberland, passed to William Watson-Armstrong. In 1903 he was created, confusingly, the 1st Lord Armstrong of the second creation – this time of Bamburgh as well as Cragside, to acknowledge the family's possession of Bamburgh Castle.

For some years the new Lord and Lady Armstrong lived in style, dividing their time between Cragside, Bamburgh and the south of France. But in due course Armstrong became involved in 'several companies of a highly speculative character'. In 1908 he faced debts of over half a million pounds. On the advice of trustees, he sold some of the finest appurtenances of Cragside, including his great-uncle's Nanking porcelain, his celebrated prize herd of shorthorn cattle, and the pick of the Cragside pictures, among which were works by

Cragside from the south with observatory dome on Gilnockie Tower; by W. L. Wyllie c.1884 (Newcastle City Library)

The 1st Lord Armstrong of the second creation (far left) with Yorisada Tokugawa, uncle of the Empress of Japan, behind, and other guests at Cragside in 1929

Constable, Turner, Cooke, Millais, Leighton and Albert Moore (see Chapter Four). Thereafter life at Cragside assumed a less lavish character. Since 1900 the house appears to have undergone few structural alterations.

The 2nd Lord Armstrong of the second creation, the proprietor of Cragside after his father's death in 1941, died in 1972. With the death of the 3rd Lord Armstrong in 1987, the title finally lapsed. In 1977 the house, with the 911 acres around it forming the present country park and two farms in the Coquet valley, passed to the Treasury in part settlement of death duties incurred on his estate. It was then transferred to the National Trust through the auspices of the National Land Fund, aided by a generous gift from the 3rd Lord Armstrong. Substantial help was received from the Historic Buildings Council during the long restoration that followed, which was supervised by the architects Mauchlen, Weightman and Elphick of Newcastle in close collaboration with Sheila Pettit, the National Trust's Historic Buildings Representative for the Northumbria Region. The house was first opened to the public in 1979. Since then much has been done at Cragside, which draws an increasing number of visitors. Armstrong's many hydroelectric schemes on the estate have been revived, the rockery replanted, and in 1991 the formal terraced gardens, glasshouses, the original agent's house, and other buildings and parkland were acquired.

NOTES

1 *Newcastle Daily Chronicle*, 25 November 1888.

2 Id.

3 Peter McKenzie, *W. G. Armstrong*, 1983, p. 25.

4 D. D. Dixon, *Upper Coquetdale*, 1903, pp. 439ff.; M. D. Noble, *A Long Life*, 1925.

5 *Newcastle Daily Chronicle*, 25 November 1888.

6 Dixon, op. cit., p. 440.

7 *Newcastle Daily Journal*, Supplement for Royal Visit to the North-East, 1884, p. 150.

8 Id.

9 Andrew Saint, *Richard Norman Shaw*, 1976, pp. 67–9; the full text of the letter is given in *Architectural History*, xviii, 1975, p. 63.

10 Reginald Blomfield, *Richard Norman Shaw, R.A.*, 1940, p. 20.

THE ARMSTRONG AND WATSON-ARMSTRONG FAMILY

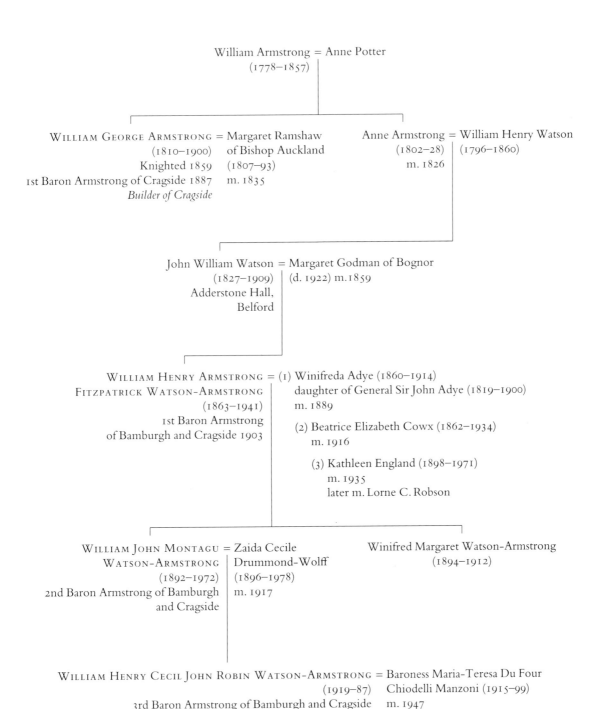

William Armstrong = Anne Potter
(1778–1857)

WILLIAM GEORGE ARMSTRONG = Margaret Ramshaw
(1810–1900)   of Bishop Auckland
Knighted 1859   (1807–93)
1st Baron Armstrong of Cragside 1887   m. 1835
Builder of Cragside

Anne Armstrong = William Henry Watson
(1802–28)   (1796–1860)
m. 1826

John William Watson = Margaret Godman of Bognor
(1827–1909)   (d. 1922) m. 1859
Adderstone Hall,
Belford

WILLIAM HENRY ARMSTRONG = (1) Winifreda Adye (1860–1914)
FITZPATRICK WATSON-ARMSTRONG   daughter of General Sir John Adye (1819–1900)
(1863–1941)   m. 1889
1st Baron Armstrong
of Bamburgh and Cragside 1903   (2) Beatrice Elizabeth Cowx (1862–1934)
m. 1916

(3) Kathleen England (1898–1971)
m. 1935
later m. Lorne C. Robson

WILLIAM JOHN MONTAGU = Zaida Cecile
WATSON-ARMSTRONG   Drummond-Wolff
(1892–1972)   (1896–1978)
2nd Baron Armstrong of Bamburgh   m. 1917
and Cragside

Winifred Margaret Watson-Armstrong
(1894–1912)

WILLIAM HENRY CECIL JOHN ROBIN WATSON-ARMSTRONG = Baroness Maria-Teresa Du Four
(1919–87)   Chiodelli Manzoni (1915–99)
3rd Baron Armstrong of Bamburgh and Cragside   m. 1947

CHAPTER THREE
ARMSTRONG THE INNOVATOR

In arguing against nineteenth-century patent law, William Armstrong dismissed the importance of invention, stating that:

Mere conception of primary ideas in invention is not a matter involving much labour and, it is not a thing . . . demanding a large reward; it is rather the subsequent labour which the man bestows in perfecting the invention . . .[1]

We now refer to the 'subsequent labour' as innovation and Armstrong's argument was a reflection of his lifelong success as an innovator. He was supremely gifted at bringing good scientific ideas,

his own or other people's, to the market-place. And he reaped the rewards for doing so, making fortunes as a result of his innovations in hydraulics and ordnance.

HYDRAULICS

Armstrong's first attempt at innovation was his only failure. He noticed that waterwheels used only a fraction of the energy of the water available to them, and in 1839 he built an 'improved hydraulic wheel' to overcome the deficiency. The device used ingenious solutions to difficult technical problems,

An electrical discharge photographed by John Worsnop for Armstrong's 'Electric Movement in Air and Water' (1897)

but the materials available at the time were in-adequate. In particular, the leather seals leaked and deteriorated quickly. As the prototype also lacked power, Armstrong was unable to arouse industrial interest.

In 1844–5 Armstrong was the driving force behind the formation of the Whittle Dene Water Company, which was established to provide New-castle with a new, clean supply from reservoirs in the hills. The Whittle Dene reservoirs were 200 feet above sea level, and Armstrong knew that this head of water would be sufficient to power hydraulic machines in the city. As soon as the water supply was available, he approached Newcastle City Cor-poration with a proposal to install cranes of his own design in the docks. The new cranes relied on the hydraulic multiplying sheave or 'jigger', which uses

the well-tried principle of the block and tackle to magnify the limited movements normally associ-ated with hydraulic power. They were a great success and led to the formation of the Newcastle Cranage Company in 1846. A year later Armstrong was able to buy land at Elswick near the River Tyne to build a factory for the newly formed W.G.Arm-strong & Company.

Hydraulic machines could not be operated in areas where there were no water mains or the mains were of low pressure. In 1849 Armstrong built the 200-foot-high Grimsby Tower to solve the prob-lem. At the top of the tower was a tank of water which provided a working head for dock machin-ery. This arrangement also eliminated fluctuations in the mains pressure caused by varying demand, a problem in Armstrong's earlier installations.

Armstrong's hydraulic crane, first used in the Newcastle docks in 1846

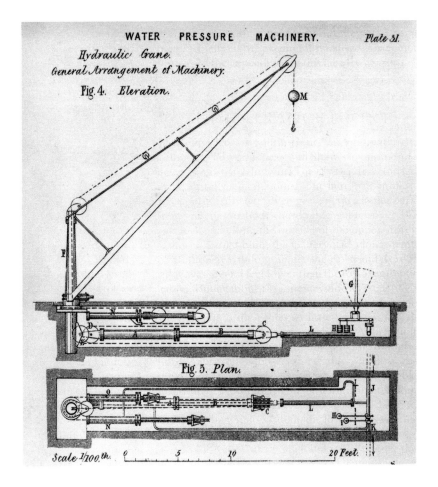

Although effective, such towers were costly to construct. They were soon superseded by the hydraulic accumulator, which provided water from a cylinder pressurised by a weighted piston. Like many of Armstrong's 'inventions', the accumulator was based on an earlier idea – Joseph Bramah's beer engine. The first hydraulic accumulator was built at New Holland in 1850 for the Manchester, Sheffield & Lincolnshire Railway. It powered five cranes with water at a pressure of 600 pounds per square inch. The accumulator paved the way for the hydraulic supply companies of the late nineteenth century, which offered a serious alternative energy source in several major cities. The London Hydraulic Power Company was formed in 1884, and at its peak in 1927 operated 184 miles of mains, supplying 8,000 machines with water at up to 850 pounds per square inch. The company ceased operation in 1976, but a number of its handsome pumping stations, like that on Wapping Wall, still survive.

Hydraulic power came a little too late to offer a realistic challenge to electricity, which provides energy in a more flexible and mobile form. Nevertheless it remains the favoured method in self-contained units where robustness, reliability and cheapness are important, for example in the braking system of a car. That this is still the case owes much to Armstrong's early innovations.

ORDNANCE

In the mid-nineteenth century there was an enormous gulf between the efficiency of artillery and smaller weapons like rifles and pistols. Military conservatism and financial restrictions meant that the British Army went into the Crimean War in 1854 with the same weapons it had used at Waterloo 40 years earlier. Field guns still had bronze or cast-iron smooth-bored barrels and fired round, cast-iron shot loaded via the muzzle. The explosive charge was ignited through a small hole or vent at the back of the barrel by a lighted match held in a long staff. By contrast, the commercial market's demand for sporting pieces had stimulated the development of more sophisticated small arms. The best small arms had rifled wrought-iron barrels, breech-loading mechanisms, multiple action and

percussion ignition. These refinements meant that rifles often had a greater range than artillery.

Armstrong's innovation was to apply the advanced features of small arms to the manufacture of artillery. At the same time he demonstrated his practical genius in overcoming the considerable technical problems faced in making these features work on a much larger scale. Armstrong's new artillery barrel consisted of a wrought-iron or steel tube spiral-wound with wrought-iron bar, which combined overall lightness with strength at the breech. The inner tube was machined with 'poly-groove rifling', spiral grooves which imparted spin to the projectile to improve range and accuracy. The breech-loading mechanism consisted of a removable vent piece held in place by a hollow screw through which the gun was loaded. Loading from the breech like this was quicker, more convenient and safer for the gun crew.

Armstrong also developed a range of cylindrical cast-iron projectiles capable of much greater accuracy and destructiveness. They were covered in soft lead, which took up the shape of the rifled barrel on firing. The extra weight of Armstrong's cylindrical projectiles compared with traditional spherical cannonballs of the same diameter increased energy and improved penetration. When a gun is fired, a chemical reaction converts the energy stored in the explosive charge to high-pressure gas which forces the projectile out of the barrel. The prevention of gas leakage increases the velocity and therefore the energy and range of the projectiles. Armstrong's projectiles had a hollow base which expanded to form a gas-tight seal. The breech was sealed by lining it with copper rings.

A small prototype, known as the Number One Gun, was successfully tested in 1855 and 12- and 18-pounder versions soon followed. In 1858 comparative trials proved Armstrong's gun was superior to its competitors, and it was adopted by the military. Armstrong went on to design larger versions, and in 1859 the Elswick Ordnance Company was formed to manufacture the weapons.

In 1869 the military reverted to muzzle loaders, perhaps because of a number of accidents caused by incorrect closure of the breech. Ten years later new gunpowders greatly increased performance but required guns with longer barrels. These were difficult to load via the muzzle and so an improved breech mechanism was developed. The future of one of Armstrong's greatest innovations was secured.

CONSERVATION AND ALTERNATIVE TECHNOLOGY

Armstrong was at the forefront in establishing Britain's industrial base, but he also took a pioneering interest in environmental issues. His ideas on the production, use and conservation of energy were a long way ahead of his time. They are even more appropriate now, in a world where demand for energy continues to increase amid growing concern for the proper use of the Earth's natural resources.

In 1855 the Northumberland Steam Collieries Association (NSCA) asked Armstrong to join a team of scientists to study the performance of the region's coal. The project arose because the Royal Navy had switched to Welsh coal in its steam-powered ships, claiming that it gave more energy and produced less smoke that might betray a ship's position and obscure signalling. The loss of an important consumer like the Royal Navy would have been a major blow to the economy of this coal-producing region. By 1858 the team had shown that the local coal performed as well or better than Welsh coal in all respects. The work alerted Armstrong to the need for conservation, and he complained that coal was used 'wastefully and extravagantly in all its applications'.[2] In 1863 he went on to predict that 'England will cease to be a coal producing country . . . within 200 years'.[3]

The NSCA project also strengthened Armstrong's belief in water power as an alternative to steam, and his company began manufacturing a wide variety of water-powered machines for industry. Later, as president of the British Association for the Advancement of Science, he predicted the widespread use of hydroelectricity, stating that 'whenever the time comes for harnessing the power of great waterfalls the transmission of power by electricity will become a system of great importance'.[4]

Armstrong's interest in alternative energy went beyond the use of water power. He calculated that 'the solar heat operating on one acre in the tropics would . . . exert the amazing power of 4000 horses acting for nearly nine hours every day',[5] and he suggested that the 'direct heating action of the sun's rays' might be used 'in complete substitution for a steam engine'.[6] He also talked about wind, tidal and chemical energy.

TECHNOLOGY AT CRAGSIDE

Armstrong used his water-powered machines at Cragside to help with the domestic chores and to impress prospective customers and visiting dignitaries. The Cragside installations led the house to be described as the 'palace of a modern magician', but it was really Armstrong's shop window and research laboratory. Many of his installations survive and can be seen on the Power Circuit, a circular walk through the house and grounds.

WATER SUPPLY

In 1865 the Debdon Burn, which runs through the valley below the house, dried up and there was a shortage of water at Cragside. To prevent this occurring again, Armstrong built a dam to store water in what became Tumbleton Lake.

The 35-foot head of water created by damming the stream was used to power a hydraulic engine installed in 1868 in a small stone-built Pump House. This drove a pair of pumps which took spring water from a tank on the roof of the building to a reservoir 200 feet above the house. The water then flowed by gravity into the house where it was used for domestic purposes and to power labour-saving machines, including a hydraulic lift, a spit in the Kitchen, and laundry equipment.

Water from Tumbleton Lake entered the hydraulic engine through a valve and forced a piston to move in a cylinder. At the end of each stroke the valve gear operated to reverse the piston. Water which had done its work was exhausted into Debdon Burn through a tailrace, while a new supply of water was admitted to the other side of the piston. The pumps were driven directly by the piston and delivered fresh water to the reservoir above the house with each stroke of the engine.

The speed of the engine was controlled up to a maximum of one stroke every 20 seconds by a valve on the engine's water supply. A float mechanism in the roof tank opened or closed the valve according to the availability of spring water.

The storage reservoir above the house is also of interest. It was designed to encourage the settling of any solid material that had been carried up in the supply. Water enters the conical reservoir tangentially so that a whirlpool effect is created. This causes

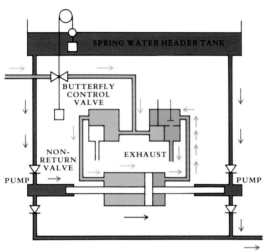

First stroke

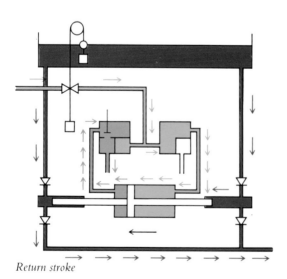

Return stroke

particles to migrate to the edge of the reservoir tank where they roll down the sloping sides to the bottom. Clear water for use in the house is drawn from the top of the tank.

HYDRAULIC LIFT

A hydraulic passenger lift was installed in the house between 1870 and 1880. It worked between the basement and the second floor and was used mainly by the domestic staff, for example to take coal to the open fires in rooms on the upper floors. Armstrong's lift removed this exhausting and hitherto unavoidable chore of household life.

The Cragside lift employed on a smaller scale the hydraulic technology which Armstrong had developed so successfully to power the cranes in the Newcastle docks. It was controlled by a 'jigger', a movable ram or piston in a fixed cylinder fitted with a system of pulleys. In this case the cylinder contains two rams, set one within another. This arrangement was designed to enable cranes to cope with a wide range of loads. For heavy loads, the two rams worked together as one. For lighter loads, the larger ram was locked in position, while the smaller ram dealt with the load by itself. In this lift installation, the larger ram was permanently locked in position, suggesting that Armstrong had adapted an off-the-shelf item rather than used a purpose-built machine.

The lift was operated in this fashion. Water fed in from the reservoir above the house forced the ram through the cylinder. A chain running over the pulley system and attached to the lift cage ensured that the ram needed to move only 5 feet to carry the lift up the 30-foot shaft. The force of $8\frac{3}{4}$ tons generated by the ram was sufficient to cope with any reasonable load. Passengers operated the lift by pulling a rope in the compartment in the direction they wished to travel. This was attached to valves on the cylinder, which allowed water in to raise the lift, and out to lower it. A projection on the ram connected to these same valves made sure that the lift stopped automatically at the basement, ground and second floors. The manual rope system was also used to call the lift. A handle was fitted to the control rope at each floor and there was an indicator which showed which way to move it to call the lift.

A hydraulic lift linked the Scullery in the basement with the Kitchen above so that heavy cast-iron pots and pans did not have to be carried up and down the stairs by hand

Armstrong's 'hydroelectric' machine was designed to generate static electricity. It began his lifelong interest in electricity

The hydraulic lift was replaced by an electric version in the same shaft in 1945, but the jigger can still be seen in the basement.

ELECTRICITY

One of Armstrong's first encounters with electricity was in 1840 when he heard that a jet of steam issuing from a boiler at the local Cramlington colliery was giving the operators electric shocks. He discovered that this was due to static electricity produced by the friction of water droplets on the boiler body as they were swept out by the steam. By 1842 Armstrong had built a powerful electrostatic generator based on what became known as the 'Armstrong Effect'. This 'evaporating apparatus' or 'hydroelectric machine' (as it was somewhat misleadingly called) was responsible for his election as a Fellow of the Royal Society in 1846.

The evaporating apparatus started Armstrong's lifelong interest in electricity. He was to concentrate on the practical use of current electricity for lighting at Cragside, but he also continued to experiment with electrostatics. His laboratory at Cragside contained many pieces of equipment to demonstrate electrical phenomena. In 1892, at the age of 82, he

31

Cragside lit by electricity; an engraving from 'The Graphic', 2 April 1881

returned to the subject with renewed vigour, publishing his earlier work on electrical discharges and conducting new experiments.

Many of Armstrong's most important innovations at Cragside combine his twin fascination with electricity and water. In 1870 he constructed Debdon Lake and Nelly's Moss Lakes to increase the potential of water power at Cragside. At Debdon he installed a Vortex turbine made by Williamsons of Kendal to drive a Siemens dynamo. This was probably the world's first hydroelectric power station. The electricity was used to light an arc lamp in the Gallery in 1878, but the arrangement was not very satisfactory because these early arc lamps were smoky, messy, unsafe and far too bright for domestic use. Shortly afterwards Armstrong's friend Joseph Swan perfected the light bulb, or 'incandescent lamp', which was more convenient to use and gave a softer light. By December 1880 some of the new lamps had been fitted at Cragside: 'the first proper installation,' said Swan.[7]

At first Swan's lamps were supplied with electricity from the Debdon installation, but as more and more lights went on at Cragside, a larger power source was needed and so Armstrong began building Burnfoot Power House. The first phase of this project was completed in 1886; it housed a purpose-built generating set supplied by Gilbert Gilkes & Company (formerly Williamsons). The new turbine took its supply from Nelly's Moss Lakes 340 feet above the Power House. It was designed to produce a maximum of 24 horsepower at 1500 rpm, to turn a Crompton direct current dynamo that generated 110 volts and 90 amps at 790 rpm.

One of the Burnfoot set's main innovative features was the self-regulating mechanism that helped to conserve water. When more electricity was required, a solenoid-operated valve opened the turbine's guide vanes to admit more water. The same valve closed the guide vanes when demand fell.

Portable batteries became available in Britain in 1883 and were soon installed in an addition to the Power House at Burnfoot to store electricity for use at times of peak demand and during breakdown and maintenance. They also helped the system respond smoothly to sudden increases in load. Another

solenoid valve in the battery circuit switched the main sluice valve on or off. This stopped the turbine automatically, to prevent overcharging the batteries, and restarted it when the battery output fell to a preset level.

By 1895 demand for electricity at Cragside had increased so much that a gas-powered engine was installed in a further extension to the Burnfoot building to drive a second generator, together with the existing Crompton generator, through the turbine. One generator could then be connected directly to the lighting circuits in regular use, such as those in the passages and below stairs, while the other could charge the batteries. Coal gas for the

In 1880 the cloisonné enamel lamps in the Library were converted to electricity, which was supplied by the generator in the grounds

engine came from the Rothbury Town Gas Works, which Armstrong founded when the engine was installed. The new generator was a Thomas Parker machine supplied by Drake & Gorham of London. It was a direct current model rated at 70 amps, 150 volts at 1300 rpm, and was ideally suited to incandescent lighting circuits. The combined system of water turbine and gas engine proved remarkably flexible, efficient and reliable. The turbine, which was not intended to drive both generators by itself, was used to supplement the gas engine to conserve fuel. The gas engine could easily cope by itself when water was in short supply.

All that remains of the gas engine is the $3\frac{1}{2}$ ton, 8-foot-diameter flywheel which has provoked much speculation. It has always been supposed that the engine was made by Tangye Brothers of Birmingham but a standard Tangye unit would have been fitted with two much smaller flywheels. Armstrong may have had the single large flywheel fitted to ensure the even running essential for electric lighting, or the engine may have come from a different manufacturer.

In about 1920 a smaller, more efficient engine supplanted the original gas engine. This no longer exists but a restored oil engine of about the same size and date has been installed to give some idea of the appearance of the set-up. This is a single-cylinder 4-stroke Ruston & Hornsby petrol/paraffin engine of 1923 with an output of 10 horsepower at 370 rpm. It came complete with its own Crompton generator and switchboard from Ightham Mote in Kent. The generator is rated at 155/110 volts, 30/40 amps at 145 rpm.

The first phase of the building at Burnfoot included an electrician's control room. Damp is a threat to any electrical equipment, and so this room was always kept warm and dry. It originally housed the equipment which controlled the turbine and the electrical output. From here the operator was in direct contact by telephone with the house and estate. Later he was also required to warn the gas works before starting the gas engine.

Mains electricity came to Cragside in 1945.

ESTATE FARMS

Armstrong did not restrict his use of innovative technology to his own home. His estate farms also benefited. At Low Trewhitt near Thropton a Vortex water turbine was supplied by Gilbert Gilkes & Company in 1883. It was installed at the bottom of a shaft and used to power belt-driven threshing and winnowing machines 40 feet above it. The turbine drew its water from a pond, which was itself supplied by a leat from a reservoir higher up the valley.

At Cragend Farm a stone-walled silo was constructed for silage making. It consists of a central tower between two cement-rendered tanks with a corrugated wrought-iron roof. A hydraulic jigger in the tower was used to raise and lower circular 1-ton weights, which compressed the silage in the tanks. This fine purpose-built agricultural building represents one of the earliest examples of silage-making, which did not become widespread in Britain until the late nineteenth century.

Many of Armstrong's other farms were also served by innovative machinery. The waterwheel pump now set up in the Visitor Centre came from Warton, and there were large turbines and silos in use on at least two other farms.

NOTES

1 Report of the Commissioners Appointed to Inquire into the Working of the Law Relating to Letters Patent for Inventions [5974], xxix, 1865.

2 Presidential address to the British Association for the Advancement of Science, Newcastle, 1863. 'The Coal Supply'.

3 Ibid.

4 Presidential address to the mechanical section of the British Association for the Advancement of Science, York, 1883. 'Utilisation of Natural Forces'.

5 Ibid.

6 Ibid.

7 J. W. Swan in a letter to John Worsnop, quoted in an article on Armstrong in the *Newcastle Daily Record*, 27 December 1900.

CHAPTER FOUR
ARMSTRONG THE COLLECTOR

Victorian visitors to Cragside were greeted by a rich array of oil paintings, watercolours, stuffed birds and shells. Such treasures were only to be expected in the home of Lord Armstrong, a man who served as President of Newcastle's Arts Association and Literary and Philosophical Society, and who was also a generous benefactor of the Hancock Museum of Natural History. Nor were contemporary viewers taken aback by the spindly, Japanese-inspired furniture in the Library, or the softly glowing stained-glass windows designed by Dante Gabriel Rossetti and produced by Morris & Company. It only stood to reason that the inventor who redefined the rules of hydraulic engineering and arms manufacturing would be uninhibited by artistic convention. But while nineteenth-century observers may have been impressed with Armstrong's boldness, from today's perspective it is evident that, in aesthetic matters at least, he was a follower rather than a leader.

The core of Armstrong's collection mirrored the tastes of the typical mid-Victorian patron which ran to modern paintings by popular British artists specialising in landscape, genre scenes and historical costume pieces. Even his more adventurous purchases reflected a pattern of collecting established by his younger business associates in the North East. Armstrong shrewdly diluted the *avant-garde* with the conservative in his home, achieving an ambience that satisfied the expectations of both his progressive

'Faithful unto Death', by H. H. Emmerson, 1874 (No. 28; Gallery), is typical of Armstrong's conservative taste. Emmerson was a Newcastle artist much patronised by him

neighbours and his more staid British and overseas guests.

Armstrong's collection was assembled and shaped in three distinctive campaigns, which parallel the course of his personal and professional life: the preoccupied years of 1854–69, followed by aggressive expansion between 1869 and 1878, and, finally, consolidation and exultation in the two decades preceding his death in 1900.

During his initial phase of collecting, Armstrong's first loyalty lay with his industrial endeavours at Woolwich and Elswick. He abjured rest, snatching naps on a camp bed in his office and resisting the temptation of holidays. The pattern of his art purchases during these hectic years was correspondingly distracted and erratic. He bought primarily from sources close to hand, from Northumbrian artists W. J. Blacklock, T. M. Richardson Sr and H. H. Emmerson, and from an assortment of local dealers. The manner in which Armstrong displayed his early possessions at Jesmond Dene suggests that he perceived his art collection as little more than a backdrop for entertaining. J. Comyns Carr recollected that he attended 'a dinner served in the great banqueting hall at Jesmond Dene, the walls of which were richly decorated with many important examples of modern art'.[1] The flickering candlelight no doubt contributed to the inability of the future director of the Grosvenor Gallery to identify any of the paintings. Cragside, however, was another matter. There Armstrong brought his acquisitions out of the shadows and, in the process, revealed more about himself.

After 1863 Armstrong found more time for his personal pursuits. He had reached a professional pinnacle that year when he was elected president of the British Association for the Advancement of Science and presided over its annual meeting in Newcastle. Yet, despite the knighthood he had received in 1859, Armstrong's success was blighted in the 1860s by criticism levelled by his gunmaking rivals and by a drastic reduction in government orders.[2] Armstrong's first years at Cragside were, therefore, a time of retrenchment and reassessment. Although he is frequently thought to have retired from work, it would be more accurate to say that he withdrew from the mundane day-to-day running of the business to concentrate on devising a long-term strategy for his industrial empire. Armstrong then turned a portion of his formidable energy toward art collecting. According to an inventory of his paintings and drawings written in his own hand around 1876, Armstrong acquired more than three-quarters of the Cragside collection in the brief period of seven years following his first purchase at Christie's in 1869.[3]

Why did Armstrong suddenly give art such a high priority? By expanding his fishing lodge into an impressive villa and adorning it with expensive pictures and artefacts, did he hope to be welcomed into the charmed circle of country gentry? A partial answer is provided by the portrait Armstrong commissioned of himself from H. H. Emmerson (No. 7, Dining Room; illustrated on back cover). It was painted in the early 1880s, shortly after his picture-buying spree had come to an end. Emmerson presents a disarmingly informal view of Armstrong, in carpet slippers, cosily ensconced in the inglenook of his Dining Room, catching up on the day's news. But a closer examination of Emmerson's painstakingly rendered environment belies the homespun ambience suggested by the motto carved on the fireplace: 'East or West, Hame's Best'. The delicately sculptured bench, hand-crafted carpet, blue-and-white china on the mantelpiece, and lustrous stained-glass windows, signify a degree of wealth that contrasts with the modesty of Armstrong's attire. Were he not so completely relaxed and so obviously the master of the dogs who await his command, we would suspect he did not belong.

Ambivalence was an essential component in Armstrong's character. Like many other members of the Victorian middle class who achieved positions of wealth and power, Armstrong wanted to preserve the independence which had won him his fortune, but also to enjoy the charms of the aristocratic way of life. His solution was to compromise. While he assumed the persona of the country gentleman to the extent that he owned a large estate, embellished his home with costly objects, and entertained lavishly, he maintained his middle-class identity by his dedication to industry and scientific innovation. Nor did Armstrong try to give the illusion of hereditary wealth by purchasing

The shells now displayed in the Gallery are a small part of Armstrong's huge collection of natural history specimens

a historic house and estate. He chose instead to construct a modern mansion with every modern convenience, albeit in an 'Old English' style.

The Cragside collection also bears the stamp of Armstrong's ambivalence. Its gilded frames and large-scale canvases signify a collector who had aristocratic pretensions. Yet the signatures affixed to these pictures were not those of the Old Masters, but belonged to living or recently deceased British artists. Too busy to indulge in the Grand Tour routinely undertaken by aspiring connoisseurs, Armstrong subscribed to the middle-class tradition of patronising contemporary British artists, which had been established in the early Victorian period by the magnates Robert Vernon and John Sheep-shanks. His purchases at Christie's in 1869 were works by J. F. Herring and T. S. Cooper, both artists popular with Vernon and Sheepshanks. The ten 6-foot canvases and the host of smaller works by such fashionable artists as Clarkson Stanfield, W. J. Müller, David Cox and John Phillip that Armstrong acquired in the 1870s were typical of the paintings sought out by mid-Victorian captains of industry.

That is not to say that Armstrong possessed no 'cultural capital'[4] of his own. Although Armstrong

was not born in luxury, his mother was reputedly 'a highly cultured woman' who saw to her son's training in aesthetic matters.[5] Another important early influence was Armorer Donkin, who was an art collector as well as family friend. This early exposure to the fine arts gave Armstrong a head start in the culture game.

When Armstrong was ready to begin collecting in earnest in the 1870s, he had ample opportunity to study the important collections of modern art assembled by the members of Newcastle's middle-class cultural élite with whom he served on civic committees, most notably Charles Mitchell, Sir Isaac Lowthian Bell and James Leathart. An insurance inventory of the works of art owned by Armstrong's business partner Charles Mitchell listed over four hundred objects.[6] These possessions were elegantly displayed in a private picture gallery in his palatial home Jesmond Towers, near Armstrong's Newcastle house. Armstrong concurred with Mitchell's patronage of popular landscapists such as A. W. Hunt and Royal Academicians such as Lord Leighton, but eschewed those French painters and British sculptors that his partner's son, artist Charles Mitchell, encouraged his father to support.

Although much smaller in size, Lowthian Bell's collection more closely resembled the aesthetic limitations Armstrong set for himself: conventional British paintings enlivened by the works of a few more enterprising spirits displayed in a series of rooms featuring the interior designs of William Morris. These two Northumbrians had other things in common: both were knighted in reward for industrial accomplishments, both constructed modern mansions on large estates, and both refused to sever their ties with industry. Furthermore, each demonstrated pride in his industrial achievements by commissioning artists to paint his factories. Lowthian Bell employed A. W. Hunt and Albert Goodwin to depict his iron foundry, while Armstrong turned to T. M. Hemy in 1886 for a painted record of Elswick Works.

Armstrong and Lowthian Bell, like many other men of their station, were partial to the art of John Everett Millais. Lowthian Bell first commissioned a work from the artist in 1865, ten years before Armstrong was to bid successfully for a pair of

*'Chill October'; by
J. E. Millais, 1870 (private
collection). Bought by
Armstrong in 1875*

pictures by Millais at auction. Both *Jephthah's Daughter* (National Museum of Wales, Cardiff), painted by Millais in 1867, and *Chill October* (private collection), created four years later, were produced after he had given up the meticulous methods and romantic themes of his early Pre-Raphaelite years in the hope of attracting well-heeled patrons by painting subjects drawn from less esoteric sources. Cotton merchant Samuel Mendel paid a record £4,200 for *Jephthah*, the highest price the artist had yet received. When financial collapse forced Mendel to sell his art collection in 1875, Armstrong was determined to possess the picture. He travelled to London in great secrecy, asking the dealer William Agnew to bid on his behalf. A measure of Armstrong's anticipation can be gleaned from a letter he wrote to his wife Margaret on the eve of the sale:

23 April 1875

My dear Margaret,

The first day's sale of the Manley Hall collection has come off today. I only bid for one picture & got it. It is a landscape by Müller not large but very fine. Price 600 gs. I reserve my strength for tomorrow when the most important pictures will be sold. I fear there will be a severe competition for Millais' *Jephthah* which is exciting great admiration. It is so very fine that I must

have it even at the £4000 which Emmerson said I would give. But whatever I give I wish to keep as secret as I can.

Yours affly
W. G. Armstrong
P.S.
Please put this note in the fire.[7]

Armstrong's letter is highly revealing because it not only shows how personally involved he was in his art collecting, but it also discloses that he was anxious to involve his wife. Margaret Ramshaw Armstrong played a more active role in creating the Cragside collection than is sometimes realised. She worked out the details of commissions with Emmerson. As a patron of the Hancock Museum of Natural History, which was founded in 1884 with the Armstrongs' financial support, she was equally keen to acquire stuffed birds for her home; several examples are the work of John Hancock, the great Victorian taxidermist. The daughter of an engineer from Bishop Auckland, she also supervised her husband's experiments in electricity in his absence. While the majority of Victorian women were inhibited by the artificial barriers separating the private sphere of the home from the public arena of work and accomplishment, Margaret Armstrong intrepidly surmounted these obstacles.

In confessing his fears about the imminent bidding war at Christie's to his wife, Armstrong gives us a measure of the importance of art in his life. Admittedly, he was clearly captivated by the competitive atmosphere of the auction house; yet, his comment about the aesthetic quality of the painting proves that he was motivated by more than mere possessiveness. Today the narrative of *Jephthah's* stagey tableau requires explanation and distracts us from an appreciation of its formal qualities. A Victorian viewer would have been more readily familiar with the verses from *Judges* (xi, 35) which Millais illustrates, describing the fatal vow Jepthah made which bound him to sacrifice his daughter. Armstrong's assessment of the picture was shared by his peers who greeted his purchase with a chorus of approval. Writing again to Margaret on the day of the sale, he proudly informed her that Cragside architect Richard Norman Shaw was 'immensely struck' with the picture.[8] Two days later, Armstrong reported with satisfaction that he had declined £5,000 for *Jephthah* from a distinguished collector. (It had cost him 3,800 guineas.)

Armstrong was equally pleased with the second picture by Millais that he purchased at the Mendel sale. *Chill October* was much praised when the artist first exhibited it at the Royal Academy in 1871. Critic F. G. Stephens considered it 'the picture which will attract most admirers'.[9] Armstrong was even more enthusiastic about the painting, telling Margaret that he considered it 'the finest landscape that has been produced in the present generation'.[10] Painted in Perth, it harmoniously blended with other paintings with Scottish motifs he owned by Edwin Landseer and Peter Graham. He gave *Chill October* pride of place in the Drawing Room Shaw added to Cragside in 1884 where we see it prominently placed on the far right of the north wall in a photograph of the room as it appeared in 1891. That was also the year that E. Rimbault Dibdin, art critic for the *Magazine of Art*, published a long two-part review of the Cragside collection, describing *Chill October* as 'the most famous landscape in the collection'.[11]

To the left of *Chill October*, on the west wall, hung *Jephthah's Daughter*, flanked by Philipp's *Spanish Flower Seller* (Aberdeen Art Gallery) and Leighton's *Noble Lady of Venice* (Leighton House),

'Jephthah's Daughter'; by J. E. Millais, 1867 (National Museum of Wales, Cardiff). Also bought by Armstrong in 1875

In 1891 the cream of Armstrong's collection was displayed in the Drawing Room

also acquired at the Mendel sale. *Chill October*'s commanding expanse is balanced on the south wall by a canvas of almost equal dimensions, Henry Nelson O'Neil's *The Last Moments of Raphael* (Bristol City Art Gallery). This arrangement is indicative of the breadth of Armstrong's taste which stretched from the realistic landscape of Millais to the exotic genre of Phillip and the historical recreations of Leighton and O'Neil.

Armstrong's broad tastes also embraced Albert Moore's *Follow My Leader* (private collection, India), which originally formed the centrepiece of the Library. In a photograph of 1891 the painting dominates the right wall with its elongated classically attired women who playfully participate in the game identified in the picture's title. The soft blue-green palette, as well as languorous poses of the models, stylistically place this composition at the heart of the Aesthetic movement. The poet Swinburne, whose relatives came from nearby Capheaton, found in Moore the visual expression of his art-for-art's sake principles. Swinburne argued that in Moore's art, 'its meaning is beauty; and its reason for being is to be'.[12] The painting was complemented by the blue-and-white Chinese pots, formerly in Rossetti's collection, which were displayed on the bookcases and mantelpiece in the Library. Armstrong noted in his inventory that he personally commissioned Moore to paint *Follow My Leader* who, according to Rossetti, carried out his contract, on the spot, at Cragside.[13] This evidence would seem to suggest that the Northumbrian tycoon was a willing participant in the Aesthetic movement.

Armstrong, however, did not venture much further along the path to aestheticism. Always hungry for new commissions, Rossetti desperately tried to interest him in purchasing a large picture, despite his low opinion of the paintings on view at Cragside. Rossetti disparagingly noted that Armstrong owned 'a huge Horsley and a huge Burchett ... so I should think the gentleman must want something *very* fine of mine to stand such neighbours'.[14] Rossetti succeeded only in selling Armstrong a small chalk drawing, *Gretchen Discovering Faust's Jewels* (Carlisle Art Gallery), in 1874,

through the dealer Murray Marks. From the same source, Armstrong bought his concluding venture into Aesthetic movement taste, Burne-Jones's modest watercolour *The Sleeping Beauty* (Manchester City Art Gallery). That this purchase was not of major importance to the collector is indicated by his misrepresenting the artist's name in his inventory twice – originally as 'Owen Jones', corrected to 'Burn Jones' (sic).[15] Although Armstrong also installed stained glass designed by Rossetti and Burne-Jones at Cragside, he seems to have been less a patron of the Aesthetic movement than a collector who wished to own representative examples of the art of his era.

The fact that a comparatively conservative collector such as Armstrong bothered to acquire

Albert Moore's 'Follow My Leader' hung in the Library in 1891

advanced art, was due to the unusually warm reception awarded to Pre-Raphaelite and Aesthetic art in the North East. William Bell Scott, in his capacity as Head of the Newcastle School of Art, had invited his Pre-Raphaelite friends to exhibit locally from the early 1850s. Scott painted the famous scenes of Northumbrian life for the Hall at Wallington in a Pre-Raphaelite style and succeeded in converting to his views the Secretary of the School of Art, lead manufacturer James Leathart, who, in turn, enthusiastically introduced other local businessmen to the merits of innovative art. Although Armstrong did not go so far as to imitate the shrine to beauty created in Leathart's home at Brackendene, he proved he was at least conversant with the latest trends.

While the scale and decor of the Library at Cragside encourages an intimacy with works of art that is one of the hallmarks of the Aesthetic movement, the Drawing Room, in contrast, is formal and rhetorical. Designed by Shaw in 1882, twelve years after he completed the Library, this enormous reception room, with its barrel vault and altarlike chimney-piece, produces a solemn and reverential atmosphere. Since Armstrong placed the gems of his collection here, we can only conclude that he believed these works worthy of veneration.

If his arrangement of paintings in the Drawing Room at Cragside looks more grandiose than in the Library, it may also be due to the fact that Armstrong, who was in his seventies when he added this room to his home, had become increasingly egocentric as he aged. A. G. Temple, director of the Guildhall Gallery, reported that when he visited Cragside in 1892, Armstrong told him that 'he owned thirteen thousand acres around his house . . . his works at Elswick extended along the Tyne then for three miles, thirteen thousand men always at work, and £28,000 paid weekly in wages'.[16] Temple paints the picture of a typical businessman turned lord of the manor. Armstrong had been elevated to the peerage five years earlier and apparently no longer bothered to keep in check the ambivalence which had always formed part of his character. Armstrong bequeathed his paintings to his grand-nephew William Watson-Armstrong, presumably in the hope that the collection would remain intact as a monument to his taste. That dream was shattered only ten years later when they were dispersed at Christie's.

NOTES

1 J. Comyns Carr, *Some Eminent Victorians*, 1908, p. 50.

2 Stafford Linsley, 'William George Armstrong, 1st Lord Armstrong of Cragside,' *Dictionary of Business Biography*, David J. Jeremy (ed.), 4 vols, 1984–6, i, p. 70.

3 Lord Armstrong, 'Inventory of Pictures', (c.1876), Natural Trust MS.

4 Pierre Bourdieu, *Distinction: A Social Critique of the Judgement of Taste*, transl. Richard Nice, Cambridge, Mass., 1984, p. 12 *passim*.

5 *Dictionary of National Biography*, xxii, p. 63.

6 Mitchell Papers (1883). Northumberland Record Office, 497/A1 (pt).

7 W. G. Armstrong to Margaret Ramshaw Armstrong, 23 April 1875, Armstrong Family Papers. I am grateful to Peter McKenzie for providing me with photocopies of letters pertaining to Armstrong's art collecting.

8 24 April 1875, ibid.

9 F. G. Stephens, 'Royal Academy', *Athenaeum*, 29 April 1871, p. 531. See also *The Times* of the same date.

10 24 April 1875, Armstrong Family Papers.

11 E. Rimbault Dibdin, 'Lord Armstrong's Collection of Modern Pictures – II', *Magazine of Art*, xiv, 1891, p. 194.

12 Algernon Charles Swinburne, *Notes on the Royal Academy Exhibition, 1868, Part II*, p. 32.

13 'Inventory of Pictures', c.1876, No. 6. See Rossetti to Charles Augustus Howell, 22 January 1873, *The Owl and the Rossettis*, C. L. Cline (ed.), University Park, Penn, 1978, No. 193.

14 Ibid. The Horsley was *Prince Hal putting the Crown on his Head* which Armstrong had commissioned for Jesmond Dene. It does not appear on his inventory, nor does any work by Richard Burchett.

15 'Inventory of Pictures,' c.1876, No. 95.

16 A. G. Temple, *Guildhall Memories*, 1918, p. 104.

CHAPTER FIVE

TOUR OF THE HOUSE

The Exterior

Cragside is set into a west-facing slope, and its site was literally hewn out of the cliff. Much excavation and blasting must have occurred to achieve the level plateau in front of the entrance. The stones from which the house is built are believed to have come from on or near the site.

The exterior of the house as it appears today is predominantly but by no means exclusively due to the work of Norman Shaw between 1870 and 1884. Its style can best be described as Free Tudor with leavenings of Old English: that is to say, it mixes motifs culled from early Tudor houses in stone with others derived from timber-framed buildings of Kent and Cheshire that Norman Shaw had studied in the 1860s. The loose but able articulation, always a feature of Shaw's early manner, is especially marked at Cragside because of the additive nature of the work. A large number of later minor changes have detracted from the coherence of the exterior.

THE GLEN FRONT

The original Cragside of 1863 (whose architect is not known) was constructed of rock-faced stones with emphasised quoins. It was a typical mid-Victorian picturesque villa, with steep gables, fretted bargeboards, pantiled roofs, and a modest tower in the middle which now forms the lower stages of the tall central tower. Some of the rugged old walling and original rough-hewn mullioned windows may still be seen at the southern end of the west or glen front, especially round the bay window to the Study. A tour of the exterior is best begun here. The northern portion of the glen front belongs to Shaw's first extensions of 1870–2. He departed only slightly from the style of the previous house, but by dressing the masonry, varying the fenestration and using plain roof tiles he produced a much livelier look. In this part of the house he avoided half-timbering and stuck to stone, relying for effect upon his tall chimneys and prominent bay windows.

Because of sporadic but incomplete alterations, the west front does not add up to a unified whole. In 1872 Shaw proposed that the older part should be completely remodelled but this was not done. He did, however, persuade Armstrong to raise the central tower and finish off with a half-timbered gable. A simple attic storey was also built on top of the old house, with half-timbering under the eaves and a large dormer window near the south-west corner. Later minor changes – and they have been many, chiefly in the placing of windows – have not improved the appearance of this façade.

THE ENTRANCE FRONT

The entrance or south front, ending with the Gilnockie Tower, is nearly all Shaw's in outline and belongs mostly to his works of 1872–4. It is coursed in beautifully cut masonry, but here half-timberwork, originally left silver-grey, plays a larger part. It is present on both the double gables over the entrance and along the outside of the upper-storey Gallery. As first built, the Gallery had a long string of mullioned windows under the eaves and its roof ridge was several feet lower than the top of entrance gables. But in about 1884 these windows were filled in with timberwork and the roof was raised to the same height as the gables. A little later, perhaps in 1887, the Gilnockie Tower was altered. As first built in 1872–4, it had been surmounted by the dome of Lord Armstrong's observatory; this was now removed and the present gable with crowning cupola substituted, according to Shaw's original intention. Changes were also made at this date and later to several of the windows along the lower stages of this front.

The entrance court is enclosed to the east by the Drawing Room wing of 1883–4. Though built of

(Left) The glen front

(Right) The north front

smooth, sheer masonry like the rest of Shaw's work it has a lead and glass roof concealed from ground level by a parapet. The wing ends in a massive chimney-breast, the southernmost feature of the house; next to it to the east, but barely visible, is the bay of Waller's Billiard Room of 1895. Another chimney is, however, also connected with Shaw's wing. This is the eccentric set of stacks that shoot out of the ground a little above and to the east of the house. They carry the flues from the heating system and from some of the rooms built into the cliff.

THE INNER COURTYARD

To the left of the Gilnockie Tower, a deeply moulded Gothic archway leads through to the internal court of Cragside, where an answering arch beneath the northern tower takes the drive out and down towards Tumbleton Lake. The court is dominated by a haphazard collection of high wings, few of which seem to belong to the house of 1863 or to Shaw's campaigns. It is conceivable that the broad areas of rather mechanical masonry with painted half-timbering were constructed in the 1880s and '90s to Lord Armstrong's own designs. At the far end the northern gateway is Shaw's, of 1874.

THE NORTH FRONT

The north front is the most altered of Cragside's three main façades. When Shaw's first extensions of 1870–2 were finished, this front consisted simply of a tall chimney-breast serving the Library close to the west angle, and next to it a two-storey crenellated bay to the Dining Room with a gable above. At this time the chimney-breast to the Dining Room inglenook, forming a short return elevation to the east, must have been prominent. Then in 1874 Shaw added the north gateway tower, linked to the Dining Room by a low and narrow corridor. By the mid-1890s much of this had been changed. The Dining Room bay had been given a third storey and a clumsy capped roof. Moreover, extra storeys built over the connecting corridor had obscured the lower stages of the Dining Room chimney-breast and detracted from the independence of the gateway tower. Further enlargements behind and to the east of this tower meant that it lost its independence still further and became integrated almost entirely into the wing which had developed around it.

45

PLANS OF THE HOUSE

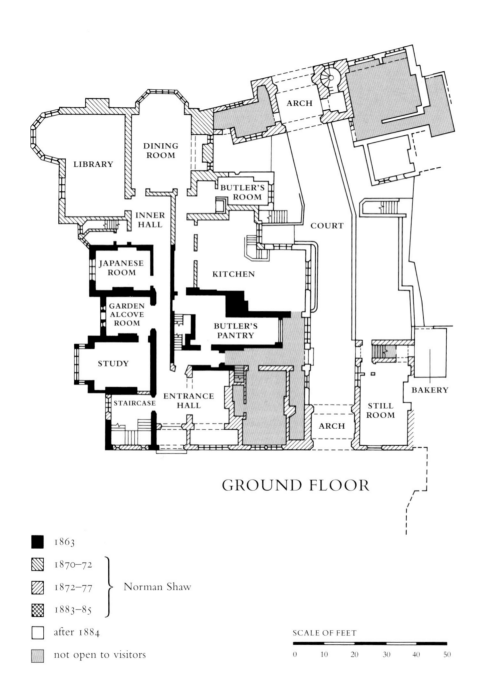

LIBRARY

DINING ROOM

ARCH

BUTLER'S ROOM

INNER HALL

COURT

JAPANESE ROOM

KITCHEN

GARDEN ALCOVE ROOM

BUTLER'S PANTRY

STUDY

STAIRCASE

ENTRANCE HALL

STILL ROOM

BAKERY

ARCH

GROUND FLOOR

■ 1863

▨ 1870–72 ⎫

▨ 1872–77 ⎬ Norman Shaw

▨ 1883–85 ⎭

□ after 1884

▨ not open to visitors

SCALE OF FEET

0   10   20   30   40   50

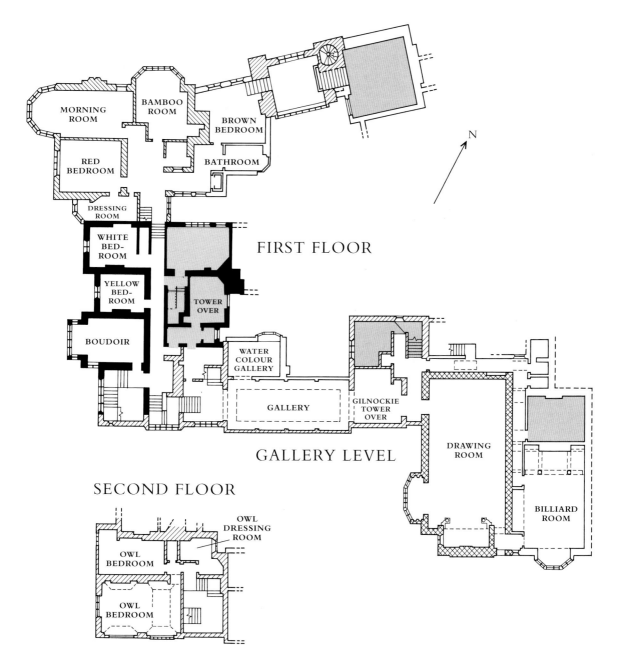

MORNING ROOM

BAMBOO ROOM

BROWN BEDROOM

RED BEDROOM

BATHROOM

DRESSING ROOM

WHITE BED-ROOM

YELLOW BED-ROOM

TOWER OVER

FIRST FLOOR

N

BOUDOIR

WATER COLOUR GALLERY

GALLERY

GILNOCKIE TOWER OVER

DRAWING ROOM

GALLERY LEVEL

SECOND FLOOR

OWL DRESSING ROOM

OWL BEDROOM

OWL BEDROOM

BILLIARD ROOM

The Interior

Because of Cragside's complicated history, its interior is additive, rambling and full of nooks and corners. The house consists of a few set pieces of great splendour, notably the Library, Dining Room and Drawing Room, and of numerous smaller and more modest rooms. They range in period from the Study, Japanese Room and Boudoir, which belong to the original house of 1863, through interiors by Norman Shaw to a medley of late Victorian apartments. Their character. tool is variable, from the heaviest 'Old English' to the whimsically Oriental.

The visitor enters the house beneath a cavernous Gothic arch near the west end of the south front, which belongs to Norman Shaw's additions of 1872–5.

THE ENTRANCE HALL

The entrance to Armstrong's original modest house of 1863 was from a porch close in position to the existing front door, but set at an angle to the building. The present Entrance Hall was formed from the original hall and a room to its east, which may have been the original servants' hall. Both were extended southwards to align with the south wall of the Staircase Hall during Norman Shaw's second campaign of extensions to the house, in 1872–4. Low and unpretentious, the Entrance Hall was originally very confined, consisting of just a short enclosed corridor. Shaw introduced two Gothic arches, scaled for social distinction, which lead off to the main and service passages. By opening the eastern wall he created a lobby overlooking the entrance court, and an opportunity to welcome visitors with a warming fire.

PICTURE

GEORGE FREDERICK WATTS, OM, RA (1817–1904)
1st Lord Armstrong of Cragside (1810–1900)
Painted about 1887, the year Sir William Armstrong was raised to the peerage as the 1st Baron Armstrong of Cragside in Queen Victoria's Golden Jubilee Honours List.

FURNITURE

A Young's weighing machine.
Two trumpet banners painted with Armstrong's coat of arms incorporating the motto 'FORTIS IN ARMIS' ('Strength in arms').
Regulator wall clock by Dent of London in mahogany and glass case.

Proceed through the right-hand arch past the back stairs (an unaltered part of the 1863 house) into

THE BUTLER'S PANTRY

This is equipped with one of the early internal telephones which were among Lord Armstrong's many innovations at Cragside. Also shown here are an early example of the Sodastream water carbonator, a linen press and two portable stoves used by shooting parties on the grouse moors.

THE BACK CORRIDOR

Although part of the original house, the corridor has suffered several changes and is now poorly lit. Here hang photographs of some former members of staff.

To the right is the Kitchen.

THE KITCHEN

A large and curious apartment of uneven height, originally less than half its present size. After 1885 it was extended to take in the old scullery and previously vacant ground to the east; a new scullery was then built beneath in the basement with connecting 'dumb waiter' lift. There is a massive 'Eagle' range by H. Walker & Son and roasting fire and ovens by Dinning & Cooke of Newcastle. In front of the fire is a wooden plate-warmer. Over the sink is a primitive early form of dishwasher, primarily intended for rinsing plates. The cook's account books are displayed in the open drawer of the kitchen table.

Steps by the left-hand window lead down to

The Butler's Pantry

THE SCULLERY AND LARDERS

The heavy cast-iron pots and pans were washed in the large sinks against the right-hand wall, and stored on the nearby racks. They could be carried up to the Kitchen immediately above in the service lift. Meat and game was hung in the adjacent larder. The present larder was originally part of a much longer corridor leading to a bigger larder cut out of the rock face. This was partially filled to support modern traffic loads in the courtyard above.

At the end of the passage is

JIGGER ROOM

On the left is a Scotch or Barker's Mill, a kind of inverted lawn spray which converts hydraulic pressure into rotary motion for the Kitchen spit above. To the right is the hydraulic ram which powered the lift. This was introduced sometime before 1880. Valves controlled the flow of water into the large piston (or jigger) which ran along the floor. This piston was connected to the lift, which ran up the shaft by a chain. A pulley system allowed easy travel between four floors.

Retrace your steps to the Kitchen, turn right into the Back Corridor, pass the lift, and go to

THE BUTLER'S ROOM

This strategically placed small room was used by the butler when on duty, providing a measure of privacy with easy access to the front door, the Kitchen, Pantry (with wine cellars below) and the Dining Room and other reception rooms.

The Kitchen

THE DINING ROOM

This is one of two main rooms on the ground floor designed and decorated by Norman Shaw as part of his first additions to the house in 1870–2. They survive in superb condition and are among the finest remaining Victorian domestic interiors in England.

DECORATION

A weightier composition than the Library adjoining, the Dining Room is characteristic of Shaw's 'Old English' manner of interior design. It is ceiled and panelled to dado height in light oak. On the northern side is a broad bay, while at the opposite end a splendid sideboard is inset between the doors. Along the other two walls James Forsyth, a favourite craftsman of Shaw's, carved the top panels of the dado with intricate reliefs of fauna and flora. The paper above, in two shades of green, has been specially made to resemble the original supplied by the London firm of Cowtan in 1872.

INGLENOOK

The undoubted climax of the room is the heavy stone inglenook. Its broad Gothic arch displays richly carved corbels and stops, with an elaborate pierced frieze above, decorated with dogs hunting among the foliage. The heavy stone apron beneath is a motif borrowed from the kitchen at Fountains Abbey in Yorkshire and sketched by Shaw in 1861.

The fireplace itself is framed by a fender and shafts of Derbyshire Russet marble with two massive corbels, one carved with cocks, the other with wolves. These support a monolith inscribed 'East or West Hame's Best' and a shelf of Red Devonshire marble. Within the hearth are multicoloured tiles, a fireback and firedogs (or andirons) of brass and iron, dated 1872 and probably designed by Shaw. On either side are stained-glass windows with figures representing the Four Seasons designed by William Morris and supplied in 1873. Beneath these are two heavy oak settles adorned with circular 'pies' (as Shaw called them). Like the sideboard, these must have been designed by Shaw and made by James Forsyth.

The Dining Room inglenook

The Dining Room

PICTURES

Five portraits introduce the Armstrong family.

BESIDE THE FIRELACE:

William Armstrong (1778–1852).
Son of a Cumbrian farmer, and father of Lord Armstrong, he was a successful corn merchant and mayor of Newcastle.

Anne Potter, Mrs Armstrong.
Daughter of a Tyneside colliery owner and mother of Lord Armstrong.
The artist for both pictures may have been James Ramsay, the prominent Newcastle painter who did paint the portrait of Lord Armstrong as a young man at the same time *c.*1830 (see Study).

WALL OPPOSITE THE FIREPLACE, FROM THE LEFT:

HENRY HETHERINGTON EMMERSON (1831–95)
William George Armstrong 1st Lord Armstrong of Cragside (1810–1900)
It shows Lord Armstrong at his most relaxed, wearing slippers, seated in the inglenook of this room and reading the paper with his dogs at his feet. The room is shown in precise detail.

Armorer Donkin
Solicitor, business partner of Armstrong and close family friend.

Anne Armstrong (1802–1828)
Lord Armstrong's sister and only sibling. She married a successful London lawyer, William Henry Watson, who helped Armstrong with his early legal career. It was their grandson who took the name Watson-Armstrong and inherited Cragside from his great uncle.

John William Watson (1827–1909)
Lord Armstrong's nephew.

THOMAS BOWMAN GARVIE
William Watson-Armstrong (1863–1941)
Dated 1901
Lord Armstrong's great nephew and son of John William Watson. Captain Watson-Armstrong is wearing the uniform of the Northumberland Hussars and is mounted on a charger. He inherited Cragside in 1900 and in 1903 was created 1st Baron Armstrong of Bamburgh and Cragside.

FURNITURE

The expanding 'Capstan' dining-table may have been made by Forsyth, but is similar to a patented design by Robert Jupe of about 1835. The armchair with a circular seat was exhibited by Jupe's firm in about 1872. The coal scuttle is an appropriate commercial product, as is the oak corner plant-stand by Howard & Sons of London. The green leather dining-chairs by Boulnois of London are probably of the 1860s, as are the Renaissance-style *étagère* and table, the latter supporting a plate warmer by W. A. S. Benson.

CERAMICS

The circular Wedgwood ceramic plaques by E. Lesore depict mythological scenes.

TEXTILES

The fitted machine-made English carpet and curtains have been in the room since at least 1891.

LIGHT FITTINGS

Armstrong's first use of incandescent lights in 1880 (see Library) included six bulbs in the centre of the Dining Room ceiling and two others on brackets.

Turn first right into

THE LIBRARY

This beautiful and unusual room has been the main living-room in the house since it was completed in 1872, as part of the fruits of Norman Shaw's first work at Cragside. It commands magnificent views over the glen, especially from the bay window at the far end, which is built out over the rock face.

DECORATION

The Library is a fascinating essay in the application of Shaw's essentially masculine 'Old English' style to a room requiring delicacy of treatment. It is panelled in light oak to a height of some five feet and has a beamed and coffered ceiling. Both features are richly elaborated; the ceiling includes walnut panels set in squares with confidently carved bosses, while the dado is finished with small relief panels of plants and leaves. These carvings, as in the Dining Room, are by James Forsyth. The upper walls are covered with the original embossed paper, now repainted in the snuff colour known to have been there in 1891. The frieze consists of small Gothic compartments

The Library with De Morgan pictures removed in 2001

between the ceiling joists. each one painted with branches and leaves on a gold ground.

STAINED GLASS

Morris & Company supplied the glass for the top lights of the bay window in 1873. It comprises two separate series:

LEFT AND RIGHT:

Four panels portraying the writers Dante and Chaucer (designed by Burne-Jones, originally for the Combination Room, Peterhouse, Cambridge, in 1865); Spenser and Milton (by Ford Madox Brown); and the classical authors Virgil and Horace (by Burne-Jones for Cragside), Homer and Aeschylus (by Burne-Jones, originally for Peterhouse in 1872).

CENTRE:

Six panels showing episodes from the life of St George. This scheme was originally devised by Rossetti in 1862.

FIREPLACE

The fireplace, made by Forsyth, has a bold and simple surround of Egyptian onyx (probably procured during Armstrong's visit to Egypt in 1872) set in a frame of Emperor's Red marble. The figures on the bright blue majolica tile-cheeks are from a design of 1852–3 by Alfred Stevens, originally intended for a Hoole & Company stove, and the steel grate was supplied by Benham & Son.

PICTURES

Following family tradition, this room has a mixture of portraits, landscapes, figure paintings and copies of old masters.

53

PORTRAITS ON THE WALL OPPOSITE THE
FIREPLACE: IN THE CENTRE, IN AN OVAL FRAME:

Margaret Ramshaw, Lady Armstrong, 1864
(1809–93)
Daughter of a Bishop Auckland engineer and wife
of the 1st Lord Armstrong, with whom she created
Cragside and its gardens.

NEXT ON THE RIGHT:

MARY LEMON WALLER
Lord Armstrong, 1898
A study of the creator of Cragside towards the end
of his life.

FAR RIGHT:

John William Watson (1827–1909) of Adderstone
Hall.
Son of Lord Armstrong's sister, father of:

ON THE LEFT:

Lord Armstrong of Bamburgh and Cragside
(William Watson-Armstrong)
Beatrice Elizabeth Cowx, Lady Armstrong (1862–
1934), second wife of William Watson-Armstrong,
by George Glenn *c.*1920.

BETWEEN THE WINDOWS:

After Raphael, *Madonna and Child and St John,*
nineteenth-century.
A typical country house old master copy.

FIREPLACE WALL, FROM LEFT:

JOHN TURNBULL DIXON
Moorland Scene, 1891
Dixon was a draper in Rothbury, and brother of the
historian David Dippie Dixon, who became Armstrong's librarian. He illustrated his brother's books
including *Upper Coquetdale* (1903) which described
Cragside.

BERNARD BENEDICT HEMY (1845–1913)
*Sailing ship towed by steam tug, c.*1880

ABOVE THE CHIMNEYPIECE:

THOMAS MARIE MADAWASKA HEMY
(1852–1937)
*Elswick Works on the Tyne, c.*1880
A large watercolour showing the extent of Armstrong's engineering works as they approached the
height of their fame.

'Italian Girl with Doves'; by Rafael Sorbi, 1866 *(No. 22;
Library)*

ON THE RIGHT:

RAFAEL SORBI (1844–1931)
Italian Girl with Doves, 1866
Purchased by Armstrong in 1869, and typical of his
taste for gentle sentimentality.

WALL OPPOSITE WINDOWS, FROM LEFT:

J. T. DIXON
Upper Coquetdale near Shilmoor, 1891

ABRAHAM VAN STRY
Dutch Cottage Interior, nineteenth-century.
Bought in 1872 and shows an old woman reading
near an open window.

THOMAS MILES RICHARDSON (1784–1848)
Coastal scene with fishing boats near Flamborough,
1840

Richardson, the outstanding North East artist of his
generation, was prominent in efforts to get public
exhibition and appreciation of art in Newcastle.

After ANDREA DEL SARTO (?)
A Renaissance Lady, nineteenth-century
Copy of sixteenth-century portrait.

JOHN WILSON CARMICHAEL (1799–1868)
Coastal Scene by Moonlight, 1840
An unusual picture by the Newcastle artist who achieved a great reputation as a marine painter in London.

Unidentified artist
Rouen street scene with great clock and fountain, 19th century

J. T. DIXON
St. Mary's Island, Whitley Bay, 1891
A view of the island before the lighthouse was built. Exhibited at the Bewick Club in 1891.

FURNITURE

The light woodwork sets off the prevailing red-brown and black tones of the furnishings. The red is chiefly confined to the three leather sofas, two chairs, the velvet curtains and the carpet; the black to some specially designed furniture.

The outstanding pieces are a set of chairs in the Queen Anne taste made of ebonised mahogany, with cane seats and leather back patches, stamped with pomegranates, and gilt. These were made by Gillow of Lancaster and presumably designed by Shaw.

The caned library chair with attached bookrest is by Holland & Sons, from a pattern first made in the 1880s; its ebonised finish reflects the fashion of the 1870s.

The square leather-topped writing-table on stout legs in the bay is stamped with Gillow's mark (No. 7885) and was once complemented by a similar longer table in the centre of the room, though this has not been rediscovered.

There are also four black corner chairs with gold-painted flowerpieces on the backs and gilt leather seats. Though these were perhaps not in the Library first, they were based on a chair in Shaw's possession and so doubtless designed by him.

Low oak bookcases with elaborate mouldings run along the main sides of the room. The sturdy mahogany portfolio stand dates from *c.*1840.

CIGAR BOX

ON TABLE IN BAY WINDOW:

Certainly in the room by 1881, this large glass and ormolu cigar box supported by bronze negroes, representing Havana, Maryland, Virginia and Brazil, then the chief producers of tobacco.

CARPETS

The large Turkey carpet, and the pieces in a similar style in the bay and at the hearth, have been in the room since at least 1891, and may be original.

LIGHT FITTINGS

Four large *cloisonné* enamel vases stand on the bookcases. These functioned at first as oil lamps, but in 1880 they were connected to Armstrong's electric generator in the grounds, and supplied with the incandescent light bulbs newly invented by Joseph Swan of Newcastle. These bulbs were concealed by globes of clouded glass; each vase stood over a small bowl of mercury with which contact was made by an insulated interior wire; the current then passed up this wire to the bulb and back through the copper sides of the vase itself. The light could be 'turned off' simply by lifting the vase away from the mercury.

The Library at Cragside was the first room in the world provided with a permanent system of incandescent electric lighting powered by a hydroelectric generator. By 1891 Armstrong had added a simple central pendant with eight bare light bulbs, but the present ornate metal lampshades here and in the bay, made by Lea, Sons & Company of Shrewsbury, were installed before 1895.

CERAMICS

The Japanese blue-and-white vases are similar to those present when the room was photographed by Bedford Lemere in 1891.

THE INNER HALL

This space, part of Shaw's additions of 1870–2, acts as a lobby to the Dining Room and Library and connects with the previously existing main corridor. It is partly panelled and partly finished in dressed masonry. On the table is an engraving showing Cragside lit by electricity.

PICTURES

Above the library door is *William Henry Watson*, Lord Armstrong's great nephew and successor. Between the Library door and that to the Turkish Baths, are elegant Georgian gentleman and lady. Above the door to the Turkish Baths is a half length portrait of a man wearing a dark cravat and coat, possibly George Cruddas, one of Armstrong's partners.

The plunge bath

FURNITURE

Round the walls is a set of red plush chairs, probably brought from the earlier Armstrong house at Jesmond near Newcastle, together with benches and a table in a mild Renaissance style.

CERAMICS

On the shelves are further Japanese *cloisonné* vases and dishes, a distinctive feature of the interior of Cragside.

From the Inner Hall a basement stair leads to

THE TURKISH BATHS

This suite of hot-air, plunge and shower baths, together with a cooling- and dressing-room, is located beneath the Library. Norman Shaw's plan for this suite was dated 5 May 1870, and although considerable alterations were made during construction, Thomas Sopwith's diary recorded that 'the Turkish Bath at Cragside was used for the first time on November 4th 1870'.

Return along the main corridor to the front entrance, passing

THE JAPANESE ROOM

This and the following two rooms were the chief ground-floor rooms of Sir William Armstrong's original house of 1863. Their small size and homely mid-Victorian appearance come as a surprise after the grandeur of the Dining Room and Library.

The Japanese Room was Sir William Armstrong's 'Business Room' in the house of 1863. The room itself is plain, though it retains its Cowtan wallpaper of 1866. The Gothic chimney-piece was inserted in the late nineteenth century. The name is taken from the nineteenth-century prints on the walls, which were given to the Armstrongs after the First World War by Yorisada Tokugawa, an uncle of the Empress of Japan and a close friend of the family. His framed photograph stands on the table in the centre. Cragside has had many distinguished Japanese visitors, notably the present Emperor in 1953, and his son, the present Crown Prince, in 1991.

FURNITURE

The ingenious oak business desk, with its multiple pigeon-holes, drawers, pull-out slides and panelled back, is Victorian, and the glazed bookcase contains a collection of Japanese objects given to the Armstrongs over the years. The splendid light fitting here was supplied by Lea, Sons & Company of Shrewsbury shortly before 1895.

The dado of majolica tiles in the ground-floor corridor

The Study

CARPET

The main carpet is a good Feraghan in the usual Herati design on a fawn ground.

THE GARDEN ALCOVE ROOM

The central of the three main ground-floor rooms of the house of 1863, which Norman Shaw later turned into a vestibule, opening it out with an arch to let in more light. On the wall opposite this opening is one of Norman Shaw's drawings for Cragside, which shows his first proposal, of 1872, for recasting the west, glen front. Armstrong was the kind of client who could not help interfering, and

Norman Shaw's original plan was later considerably revised.

Norman Shaw added the colourful dado of majolica tiles here and in the ground- and first-floor corridors.

THE STUDY

This room began as Lady Armstrong's sitting-room, but soon became her husband's study. It has a moulded plaster ceiling, a partly gilt cornice and a low chimney-piece of marbled slate. The wallpaper was supplied by Cowtan in 1866 and was painted red soon afterwards. It was overpainted in white in the 1930s but restored to its original colour in 1978, when the cornice was also stripped to reveal the decoration of 1866 which had remained intact beneath. The pendant light fittings were again supplied by Lea, Sons & Company of Shrewsbury, in about 1892–5. On the desk are one of Armstrong's microscopes and a specimen case.

PICTURES

ABOVE CHIMNEY-PIECE:

JAMES RAMSAY (1786–1854)
William George Armstrong (1810–1900)
Painted in 1831, when Armstrong was still a law student. Ramsay was a Sheffield artist who, though based in London, visited the North East professionally several times before settling in Newcastle in 1847. On loan from Vickers Defence Systems.

A number of engravings and sketches of Cragside and Bamburgh Castle (purchased by Armstrong in 1894) also hang in this room.

CARPET

The fitted Axminster carpet is made up of strips in Herati design. The two similar rugs are Hamadans from Iran.

Return to the Entrance Hall and ascend the main stairs.

the others as electric light fittings. At first they held stubby poles looped over so as to hold large clear bulbs without shades; the present ragged staffs and petal shades were probably substituted a little before 1895.

CARPET

The Durham carpet runner was made in 1978 copying the original Indian stair carpet.

SCULPTURE

JOHN BELL (1811–95)
The Slave Girl
Bronze
Bell achieved popularity with a series of figures, often including animals, in various states of distress. The fame of his best-known work, the Guards' Crimean War Memorial of 1860, in Waterloo Place, London, would have brought the sculptor to Armstrong's attention. *The Slave Girl* dates from about 1870, when the American Civil War and the publication of *Uncle Tom's Cabin* increased revulsion against slavery and deepened interest in the dignity of the persecuted slave. In an attempt to reflect this mood, Bell created a figure which is uncomfortable to modern eyes.

THE STAIRCASE

The present oak staircase, with its bulbous 'Queen Anne' balusters and its newel posts surmounted by lions carrying light fittings, probably dates from about 1876. The stair in the house of 1863 Occupied the same position. When Shaw first altered this part of the house in about 1872–4, he merely added an upper flight over the new entrance. However, he seems afterwards to have rebuilt the whole staircase in wood and entirely replanned the upper section, where he introduced majolica tiles similar to those along the ground-floor passage.

BAROMETER

Forfin stick barometer by Negretti and Zambra in metal case.

LIGHT FITTINGS

The lions on the lower flight originally bore banners to match the one which the topmost beast still clasps. But in 1880 Armstrong decided to use

THE BOUDOIR

This is again a survival from the original house of 1863, and served initially as an upstairs drawing-room. It has a plaster ceiling in compartments with a recently uncovered stencilled pattern and gilding of about 1880, and an Italianate chimney-piece of red marble. The wallpaper is a close copy of the original flock-paper supplied by Cowtan in March 1866 and subsequently painted over. It was printed from one of the firm's contemporary blocks in 1978.

PICTURES

The watercolours and drawings are some of the best in the house and include several views of Cragside. One is of the house in 1864, another as it was ten years later, showing how the building had been extended in the interval. There are also a dramatic watercolour from the glen, and Norman Shaw's original bird's-eye view perspective sketch of 1872 to show his first proposal for raising the central tower.

The Staircase

FURNITURE

The satinwood furniture in the so-called 'Adam style', which has an appropriately light character, forms an entire suite including settees and chairs, a writing-desk and table, a large glazed cabinet and the elaborate mirrored overmantel. It dates from the early 1880s and was given to the Victoria and Albert Museum (which has lent it to Cragside) by a Mrs A. M. Johns, whose father had it specially made by a London cabinetmaker. Upon completion it was exhibited in London.

CARPET

The late nineteenth-century carpet and matching rug are Indian.

THE STAIRCASE LANDING

FURNITURE

On the landing outside the Boudoir is a built-in sideboard incorporating fragments of pieces of furniture designed for the house by Shaw.

CERAMICS

ON SIDEBOARD:

Part of an elaborate, Ridgeway dinner service, a gift from a National Trust member; the remainder of the set is in the Gallery.

The first-floor passage leads, on the left, to

THE YELLOW AND WHITE BEDROOMS

None of the suite of bedrooms on the first floor bears traces internally of the hand of Norman Shaw, and they mostly show decorators' work in the full range of late Victorian styles.

The first two are family rooms which formed part of the original house of 1863. On the left, the visitor comes first to the Yellow Bedroom, which has commercial furniture in the so-called 'Quaint style' of about 1890. The Morris 'Pomegranate' or 'Fruit' wallpaper was reprinted in 1978 from original blocks of 1864.

The White Bedroom had its furniture painted a fashionable white between the world wars. The Morris paper here is 'Bird and Trellis' – again a recent reprint from original blocks of 1864; this was the firm's first wallpaper design, made by William Morris himself with help from Philip Webb, who drew the birds and insects on the trellis. The papers were replaced on the evidence of partly used original rolls of Morris paper found in the house, one dated 1864.

THE RED BEDROOM AND DRESSING ROOM

These are structurally part of Shaw's extensions to the house in 1870–2. Both rooms are as yet unrestored and retain their pale 1930s wallpaper, which was introduced when the vigorous growth of the trees started darkening the rooms. The view, shared by most of the western rooms, embraces the rockery, the pinetum and Debdon valley. Originally there were fuller vistas towards Upper Coquetdale and the Simonside hills.

The massive suite of high-quality mahogany pieces has inlaid decoration in a modified 'Adam style', of about 1880. The pelmet and coverlet of the bed are original. The tallboy in the Dressing Room is a Georgian piece, elaborated with brass handles in about 1890.

PICTURES

Steel engravings of dogs and deer, after Landseer and of Leighton's sentimental *Farewell!* fully reflect the taste of the Armstrongs, as in a different vein do the straightforward watercolours of Tyneside and English cathedrals in the Dressing Room.

CERAMICS

The washstand set in the bedroom is of Wemyss ware.

THE LANDING

At the end of the first-floor passage the landing was also formed as part of Shaw's additions of 1870–2 (the stair from here up to the second floor is undoubtedly his), but has been much darkened by later extensions to the east.

The Yellow Bedroom

PICTURE

HENRY HETHERINGTON EMMERSON (1831–95)
Foreign Invasion
Pastel

FURNITURE

Light art nouveau rush-seated chairs, a small writing-table and a central table and bookcase in satin birch, both by Howard & Sons.

CARPET

The fitted 'Durham Axminster' carpet, once widely used at Cragside, may be original to this location.

THE MORNING ROOM

The door bears the Latin motto, *Non qui rogat sed qui rogatur admitto* ('I admit not who asks, but who is asked'). This room is situated over the Library and was, when first built in 1870–2, one of Cragside's main bedrooms, with a dressing-room attached. Later on, the two were amalgamated to make a guests' sitting-room, furnished in an 1890s version of the late eighteenth-century style. Subsequently, it became known as 'Mother's Room', which may account for the Latin homily on the door – most suitable for a dowager's fastness! Between 1986 and 1991 this room was restored to its 1900 appearance through the generosity of the Durham Members' Centre. Mackays of Durham made a replica of the original carpet, which had faded and then been irrevocably dyed.

*Part of Armstrong's
collection of butterflies
is displayed in the
Morning Room*

FURNITURE

Much of the late Victorian furniture has been reassembled, notably the large painted satinwood cabinet, which appears to be a late nineteenth-century 'Sheraton' piece. The harmonium (by Felix Joubert) is dated 1904. The set of seat furniture of the 1890s, with 'Adam-style' inlay, was an appropriate gift from a member of the Trust, as is the Rockingham-style tea-set in the cabinet. Part of Armstrong's collection of exotic butterflies, framed and mounted on gilt wood, hangs on the wall to the right of the entrance door.

THE BAMBOO ROOM

The Bamboo Room is situated over the Dining Room and is almost entirely furnished with simulated bamboo furniture, most of it made by Howard & Sons of London – perhaps as a compliment to Sir William Armstrong's many Eastern clients. The wallpaper, 'Bamboo Plant', is a modern reprint and is based on William Morris's 'Willow' design. The silk patchwork quilt was a gift from a member of the Cragside Care Group, a body of volunteers who did much essential preparatory

work for the house's opening in 1979, including the making of many pairs of curtains.

Next to the Bamboo Room is a clothes closet, seen through what was originally its outside window on the left of the passage leading to the lift. The pitchpine chest of drawers is by Howard & Sons.

THE BROWN BEDROOM AND BATHROOM

These are rooms of comparatively late date, interposed between Shaw's northern gatehouse of 1874 and the first floor of his additions of 1870–2. The bathroom was canted out over open space below. In the bedroom are a fine brass bed, mahogany furniture and a *chaise-longue*, probably all of the 1890s. The framed prints on the walls are mainly of paintings from the Armstrong collection which were sold in 1910. Outside the door can be seen one of the electric 'dressing gongs' operated from the Butler's Pantry, to warn guests of approaching meal-times.

Retrace your steps along the first-floor passage and ascend the stairs.

THE STAIRCASE

The present aspect of this part of the stairs, with its handsome majolica tiles, dates from about 1876, when Shaw replanned this part of the house. The difficulties he encountered may be seen at half-landing level, where the lowest lights to the great window over the entrance with its stained glass had to be blocked to accommodate the new arrangement.

STAINED GLASS

The glass was supplied by Morris & Co. in 1873. The panels of quarry glass with flowers diagonally arranged were designed at least partly by Morris himself, and there are sunflowers looking much like Norman Shaw's ornamental 'pies'.

One of the electric gongs used to warn guests of approaching meal-times

PICTURES

ENGLISH SCHOOL, nineteenth-century
*Newcastle Phrenological Society, c.*1840
Eight members seated at a table earnestly discussing the bumps on each other's heads. Attendants have brought glasses and decanters to aid the debate.

HEINRICH SCHMIECHEN
Head of a (blind?) lady wearing a white head dress, 1903
The subject and provenance of this picture with its elaborate leafy frame remains obscure. Schmiechen painted the full length portrait of Lord Armstrong, which hangs in the Great Hall at Bamburgh Castle.

ITALIAN SCHOOL, nineteenth-century
Nessus and Deianeira
Copy of 17th-century original.
The centaur Nessus imprudently attempts to carry off the wife of Hercules, who, as might be expected, took vigorous and fatal punitive action. Years later, Nessus achieved posthumous revenge through his poisoned cloak, causing Hercules' death. Then Deianeira committed dutiful suicide. A happy tale.

SCULPTURE

J. H. FOLEY (1818–74)
Caractacus
Bronze, dated 1862

'Pasquino'
Nineteenth-century bronze reduction of a famous Classical sculpture known in several versions, which is said to depict the Greek hero Menelaus holding the body of Patroclus after he had been killed by the Trojan Hector.

A short stair on the left, at the head of the main staircase, leads upwards to

THE 'OWL ROOMS' OR 'GUEST CHAMBERS'

These rooms are directly under the gables of the south-west corner of the house, and their unusual panelled ceilings reflect the shape of the pitched roofs above. They were built as part of Shaw's work of 1872–4. The larger, where the date 1874 was found beneath the wallpaper, overlooks the entrance front. At an early stage Shaw and Armstrong planned that this should be a billiard-room, with a high west-facing window, two windows towards the front (one is now blocked) and a vigorous stone

The Owl Bedroom

fireplace. But there is no proof that it was used as such. In the event these rooms became the Armstrongs' guest chambers. It was in this suite that the Prince and Princess of Wales lodged on their visit to Cragside in August 1884. The third small back room was either a dressing room or box room.

DECORATION

Both rooms were restored in 1980–1 and the walls covered with a reprinted paper as near as possible to that chosen in 1884, when they were redecorated for the royal visit. The ceilings and also the small water closet next to the rooms have versions of an earlier Morris 'Venetian' paper, again close to the original found here during recent restoration.

FURNITURE

The bedroom has built-in cupboards, a plumbed-in washstand and a splendid bed designed by Shaw in American black walnut with owls at the foot and a grand half-tester over the head. A photograph shows it before restoration in 1977. The dressing-room has a smaller bed with four owls, another plumbed-in washstand and a sunken bath. The rooms were furnished with some fine pieces in oak and American black walnut, designed by Norman Shaw and probably executed by W.H. Lascelles, who often worked with him at this time and may also have been responsible for the Staircase.

THE GALLERY

As now laid out, this consists of a picture and sculpture gallery in the form of a broad top-lit corridor leading to the Drawing Room, and the smaller Watercolour Gallery off to one side. These rooms appear to have been constructed in about 1872–4, and altered more than once during the 1880s. Though the underlying structure is Shaw's, none of the features now visible accords particularly with what is known of his work, apart from the stained glass at the landing. This was supplied by Morris, in 1873, and incorporates birds and butterflies designed by his architect friend Philip Webb.

When Shaw first built this part of the house in 1872–4, the Gallery was earmarked as a 'museum' or repository for Sir William Armstrong's scientific, geological and natural history specimens. It was a virtual cul-de-sac leading only to the Gilnockie Tower, where he had an observatory. Together, the museum and observatory must have formed a private wing for Armstrong's studies away from the rest of the house. The museum was essentially the same structure as the present Gallery, but its roof was supported by open iron stanchions. There was a run of windows along the south side overlooking the entrance front (now mostly blocked). Beyond, the observatory was a high, square room, lit from a dome above and from 'a large coloured window' at the further end.

By 1879 the museum had become the Gallery and boasted the best of Armstrong's pictures. It was here that an arc light powered by a hydroelectric generator was installed in 1878. This was replaced two years later with twenty of Joseph Swan's incandescent light bulbs. With the addition of the Drawing Room in 1883–4, the Gallery became a rather superior passage; the windows were blocked off and the roof was altered to improve the lighting. Probably in 1889 the ironwork of the stanchions was boxed in with light woodwork ornamented with stencil patterns. The unusual mottled dado perhaps dates from the same time, but the flock-paper is that supplied by Cowtan in 1874 now repainted to its original shade of dark red.

PICTURES

The arrangement here follows the original, with large paintings on the right hand (south) wall, and smaller ones to the north. All the pictures on the side walls of the Gallery are by the prominent Northumbrian artist, Henry Hetherington Emmerson (1831–1895), whose sentimental child portraits, animal studies, landscapes and historical romances, and fashionable Victorian interest in tragedy and death, appealed to Lord and Lady Armstrong.

ON THE LEFT WALL BENEATH THE SKYLIGHTS, FROM THE LEFT BAY:

HENRY HETHERINGTON EMMERSON (1831–95)
Orphan of the Storm, 1875
Bleak winter snow with a lamb beside its dead mother.

Silky or *Waiting for Orders*, 1874
Lord Armstrong's favourite Border Collie lies on a stony hillside, head down in an alert position.

Winter Landscape, 1875
A shepherd and his wife mounted on one horse, helped by a dog, drive a flock of sheep into a snow storm.

Bamburgh Castle, 1889
A view from the coast to the north, with a rocky beach in the foreground. The picture was painted six years before Armstrong bought Bamburgh Castle with the intention of turning it into a convalescent home for wounded service men. Much rebuilt, the castle became, and still remains, a family home. The picture was purchased in 1995.

Two Shorthorn Calves, 1874
With the growth of his estate in Coquetdale, Armstrong took an interest in improved breeds, though the picture is entirely decorative. For a long time the picture and its pair *Silky* were hung over the Dining Room doors.

ON THE RIGHT WALL, FROM THE LEFT:

HENRY HETHERINGTON EMMERSON (1831–95)
A Young Girl with Flowers, 1876
Emmerson had several daughters who were often his models. While the Armstrongs had no children of their own, their collection included several pictures of children.

Faithful unto death, 1874
In this enormous pastel, Emmerson makes the most of a melancholy local tragedy in which a shepherd died in a blizzard. The unfortunate man lies on his back, grey with frost; his anxious collies howl and snuffle, but will not leave him. Enough to make Victorian tears flow.

Gilnockie Tower in 1530, 1880.

Lord Armstrong, in search of ancestry, implied some kinship with Johnnie Armstrong of Gilnockie, a notorious border reiver (bandit), who, with forty-eight of his clan was executed at Hawick on the orders of James V in 1530. Unaware of this fate, Armstrong and his reivers are shown returning to admiring dependants at Gilnockie at the end of a successful raid. Emmerson's depiction of the tower was based on the surviving original near Langholm, which gave its name to Cragside's own Gilnockie Tower at the end of the Gallery.

Edith Emmerson: Aged Three, 1874.

Armstrong bought this portrait from the artist in the year it was painted for 100 guineas.

AT THE END OF THE GALLERY:

Portraits of the second, third and fourth owners of Cragside by George Harcourt.

ON THE RIGHT:

Portraits of William Watson Armstrong, second owner of Cragside and his second wife, Beatrice. On your left is Katherine, his third wife. There is also a haunting, posthumous portrait of the third owner (1892–1972) by Bernard. The young boy is the fourth owner, the late and last Lord Armstrong (1919–1987).

TAXIDERMY

Several birds, very fashionable in Victorian times, some mounted by John Hancock.

SCULPTURE

The sculpture includes two marble busts of Sir William Armstrong by Alexander Munro and a Parian-ware figure of a young girl. Youth and age are also represented in the other piece.

FURNITURE

Furniture includes four ebonised cabinets with gilt ornament containing a large and interesting collection of shells, a pair of sofas (a third is in the Watercolour Gallery) and a table with a marble top. All these pieces are attributable to Gillow & Company and probably date from the 1870s.

THE WATERCOLOUR GALLERY

The Watercolour Gallery has been repainted dark green on the basis of scrapes and the dado, has been restencilled from a pattern found behind the radiator. The watercolours include works by T. M. Richardson, Clarkson Stanfield and others. There is also a beautiful book of watercolours by H. H. Emmerson and J. T. Dixon, presented to the Armstrongs by the people of Rothbury to commemorate the royal visit in 1884. The gilt 'Gothic' chair was upholstered in needlework by Dorothy Watson, sister of the 1st Lord Armstrong of Bamburgh and Cragside. The Blüthner grand piano of 1913, presented by Mr and Mrs W. Smith in 1988, is used for concerts in the Gallery.

THE DRAWING ROOM

This is Shaw's last and grandest addition to Cragside, begun in 1883 and completed just before the royal visit in August of the following year. It is the only room of any size in the south-east wing, being built up over a massive system of central-heating pipes. Radically different from the Library and Dining Room, the Drawing Room is typical of Shaw's more opulent interiors of the 1880s, and had a close counterpart in his picture gallery at Dawpool, Cheshire, built in 1882–4 and since demolished. Armstrong hung the finest of his paintings in this room, including Millais's celebrated *Chill October*, sold with much of the Armstrong collection in 1910.

The ceiling has always been off-white, but the walls were restored in 1977–8 following a massive outbreak of dry-rot, using a dark-red damask based on an original perhaps supplied by Heaton.

CHIMNEY-PIECE

The showpiece of the Drawing Room is the great inglenook chimney-piece which almost fills the south wall. Designed in an early Renaissance vein by W. R. Lethaby, Shaw's brilliant chief assistant at this period, it weighs 10 tons (according to D. D. Dixon) and is made of Italian marbles, exquisitely carved by the firm of Farmer & Brindley. The inglenook within is lined in further fine marbles, with settees covered in red leather on either side. Only turf burned within the grate here in the 1st Lord

The Drawing Room

Armstrong's time. The smoke from this and other fireplaces was drawn underground to escape from a chimney disguised as a rock pile high up the hillside. To the right, the massive arch leading through to the bay is made from streaky sandstone quarried within the Cragside grounds.

PICTURES

The general arrangement here follows that of the 1880s when the room was completed. The north wall, opposite the chimneypiece, however, is occupied by three family portraits, which have hung there since the rearrangement that followed the sale of 1910.

WALL OPPOSITE THE CHIMNEYPIECE:

Three portraits by MARY LEMON WALLER (active 1871–1916) of *Winifreda, wife of Armstrong's great nephew*, 1905; and her two children, *Winifreda Watson-Armstrong* (1894–1912), and *William John*

Montagu Watson-Armstrong, later Cragside's third owner (1892–1972), 1902.

EAST WALL (OPPOSITE ENTRANCE DOOR) FROM LEFT:

W. J. MULLER
River Scene with children, 19th century

ENGLISH SCHOOL, nineteenth-century
Landscape with river, bridge and castle

JAMES FRANCIS DANBY
Landscape at Sunset with river, boats and castle, 1855

F. SHORE
Landscape near Tangiers with road, cattle and figures, 1855

CHARLES JONES
Highland Cattle in mountainous landscape, 1865

HERBERT THOMAS DICKSEE
After Chevy Chase, 1894
A fallen knight on the Field of Chevy Chase or Otterburn in 1388, with dogs howling and snuffling in proper sorrow. This enormous picture, given to

Cragside in 1977, would surely have caught Lord Armstrong's eye had he not completed his serious collecting a little earlier.

CHARLES NAPIER HEMY
Coastal scene with fishing boats at anchor, 1892

JOSEPH PETTITT
The Thames near Windsor, 1849
This somewhat dramatised version of the actual topography was bought by Armstrong at Christie's in 1869/70 in the belief that it was by T.S.Cooper.

EDWARD TRAIN
Mountainous landscape with highland loch, mid-nineteenth-century.

THOMAS DANBY
Mountainous landscape with lake and cattle, 1853
In the foreground, a figure (the cattleherd?) snoozes in the bracken.

W. DE FLEURY
River with watermill and village beyond, 1864

CHIMNEY WALL:

Two small figure pictures over the flanking doors.

LEFT:

Lady wearing lace bonnet and white dress with window and landscape, nineteenth-century.

RIGHT:

MISS F. WESTPHAL
A Holstein Peasant Woman, 1867

WINDOW BAY WALL, FROM LEFT:

EDWARD PATRY
Only an Orange Girl, 1885
The best example still at Cragside of the Armstrongs taste for somewhat sentimental pictures of children. The girl in a straw hat has the healthy complexion to be expected of a youngster who, without obvious effort, holds a basket of oranges big enough to tax a grown man.

IN THE MANNER OF GEORGE ROMNEY
Miss Stopford, c.1780
A decent, full-length, life-size portrait of a young woman in a wide hat, seated beneath a tree. The sitter was the grandmother of Winifreda Adye, the 1st wife of William Watson-Armstrong, great nephew of Lord Armstrong.

(Left) 'Undine'; by Alexander Munro (Drawing Room)

WALTER HORSLEY
The Water Seller, mid-nineteenth-century
A Moorish street scene with a water seller greeting a man and a child seated on a donkey. This may have been a memento of Lord Armstrong's visit to Egypt in 1872.

SCULPTURE

ALEXANDER MUNRO (1825–71)
Undine
Marble
The water nymph Undine, who accidently drowned her errant husband with an embrace, was the subject of several nineteenth-century romances. The figure, which can be rotated on its stand, shows Munro's virtuosity of technique and balance: the front foot barely touches the lilies. Another version of the figure in the collection of Dr Heaton, the brother-in-law of J.Aldam Heaton, Shaw's favourite decorator of the 1880s, who was probably responsible for much of the Drawing Room's original appearance. Heaton may have been the contact between Armstrong and Munro.

FURNITURE

The settees and chairs may also have been designed by J.Aldam Heaton. Together with a large inlaid cabinet and a writing-table *en suite*, these appear to be part of the original group and exhibit Arts and Crafts and Georgian features. The settees and armchairs have been re-covered. The remaining furniture is also in a modified late eighteenth-century manner. The Bechstein grand piano of 1901 was bought by the Armstrongs and has a matching pianola with a key-striking mechanism.

CARPET

The vast fitted Axminster is original to the room; once rich in colour with reds and blues, it has faded to an orange-brown and green.

CASKET

ON CENTRAL TABLE:

A casket surmounted by the figure of Charity, and decorated with Newcastle scenes. Made of Roman oak from the foundations of Pons Aelius, it was presented to Armstrong with the Freedom of the City in 1886.

The Billiard Room

THE BILLIARD ROOM

In 1893 a room hereabouts functioned as a laboratory, where Armstrong performed his late experiments on high-tension current. But in 1895 he commissioned two rooms, a Billiard Room and an 'Electrical Room' (later a Gun Room), from the architect and artist Frederick Waller of Gloucester, whose wife Mary Lemon Waller painted Armstrong in 1898 (No. 15; Library).

The Billiard Room has a south-facing bay, but, like many of the rooms at Cragside, is also top-lit. Its 'Jacobean' details, fireplace and furnishings make it an unusually complete late Victorian interior.

PICTURES

EAST WALL OPPOSITE ENTRANCE DOOR:

THOMAS BOWMAN GARVIE
1st Lord Armstrong of Bamburgh and Cragside, 1911
The second owner of Cragside in the uniform of the Northumberland Hussars. The Billiard Room, the larger part of an extension made to Cragside in 1895, was evidently intended for his enjoyment, rather than that of his uncle then aged 85.

FURNITURE

The billiard-table and all the fittings are by Burroughes & Watts. The two rush-seated settles by the fire are characteristic commercial Arts and Crafts pieces of about 1900, and Waller's design for the room is also hung here.

A passage leads behind the Drawing Room and back to the Gallery. From here, the visitor descends the Staircase and leaves the house by the front door.

(Right) Tumbleton Lake

CHAPTER SIX

THE ESTATE

What the Armstrongs achieved in the thirty years following their arrival at Cragside in 1863 was widely regarded as miraculous. As Raffles Davison wrote for *The British Architect* in 1881:

Imagine a great hill covered from bottom to crest with huge grey boulder stones, and half way up, cut out of a steppe on the hill side, the site and placing of a building of the most picturesque kind imaginable. Then having chosen the site and placed the house, call forth your gardeners by the hundreds, and bid them make amongst and around those crags and boulders cun-

ningly-winding walks, every one formed of steps of the natural grey stone. Then bring your evergreens and rare heather by the tens of thousands, plant them over and about the place till there is hardly a spot of bare soil left; then with the rarest and commonest ferns plant every crevice amongst the boulders. Form two artificial lakes in the valley near the house, so that you can defy suspicion of the manufacture. Make a carriage approach from opposite ends of the valley, so easy and pleasant that it might have been transplanted from Hyde Park; and, beside these, let there be rolling along the hill, at two heights above, carriage drives that for

views and healthful breezes shall be immaculate. Along the valley let there be a brooklet teeming with fish, and covered and bordered with trees and rocks forming a veritable glen: span the stream by rustic and iron bridges, which form the centres of a score of perfect pictures.

Yet those who knew the Armstrongs at all well, though they may have been bewildered at the scale of operations, can hardly have been surprised by the enthusiasm and energy with which they embarked upon the project. Armstrong had known and loved the area round Rothbury since his childhood. In his homes on the fringe of Newcastle he had had the opportunity to develop a taste for natural beauty, and its association with water. Pandon Dene, beside the home where he was born, was one of those narrow valleys cut by streams that make their way down to the north bank of the Tyne. Within sight of the town spires there were grassy banks, mature woodlands, and a stream big enough to turn the wheel of a corn mill close to the Armstrongs' house.

As Armstrong grew, Pandon Dene was absorbed by the growing city. Whether he was consciously aware of the loss of this boyhood haunt is not known, but that it had some effect on him is

supported by his choice of setting for his later homes. Both overlooked narrow valleys with watermills; only the scale changed.

Of Margaret Ramshaw's childhood gardens at Bishop Auckland nothing is known. Her interest in gardening becomes clear, however, after her marriage to Armstrong in 1835. They moved into a new villa at Jesmond, then Newcastle's newest and most fashionable suburb. Their villa, called Jesmond Dene, which was built on Chance Fields, has now disappeared under a second wave of urban development. All that survives of its immediate garden is an oak tree planted by the Armstrongs to celebrate their marriage, but close by there is much more lasting evidence of the Armstrongs' gardening genius. Gradually in the mid-century Armstrong was able to acquire the length of the Dene itself, including the old watermill. Here they created, though on a grander scale, something of the enchantment he had known as a child growing up near Pandon Dene. Screens of trees and sweeping lawns set off the excitement of the river tumbling down between the rocky pools. Even now, when the city totally encloses the Dene and after more than a century of service as a public park, the force

(Left) Cragside in the late 1870s, when Armstrong's massive planting programme was in its early stages

(Right) The single-span steel footbridge was built across the Debdon Burn between 1870 and 1875

of the Armstrongs' vision can be seen. They created a private garden which managed at once to combine variety, drama and a good measure of seclusion.

For once Margaret Armstrong steps forward from her more accustomed obscurity. It is she who shows expertise in plant management, whose taste is particularly mentioned, and she who corresponds with Mackenzie & Moncur of Edinburgh about the supply of heating apparatus for glasshouses. In a prevailing climate which tends to the convenience of praising Armstrong alone for so many achievements, it is a pity that more documentary evidence has not appeared to allow Margaret Armstrong her share of what was undoubtedly a combined effort.

For all its success, the garden at Jesmond was becoming hemmed in by the expanding city. Although Jesmond Dene remained their town home, the need for a more remote retreat became apparent; and in 1863 Armstrong decided that this should be near Rothbury. Later, absorbed by the developments at Cragside, the Armstrongs decided that the Dene should become a much-needed public park for Newcastle. The portion south of the Tynemouth road was transferred in 1880 and named Armstrong Park. The remainder of Jesmond Dene followed three years later. It was formally opened in 1884 by the Prince and Princess of Wales who planted a Turkey oak. To do so they travelled from Cragside.

According to his own account Armstrong's original intention was to build himself 'a small house in the neighbourhood [of Rothbury] for occasional visits in the summer time'. It seems doubtful whether he was ever going to be satisfied with the 'few acres of adjoining land'. Evidently the plan changed. Even as the original house was begun, Armstrong employed William Bertram as resident land steward, to share the discomfort of the tumbledown mill. If this was intended as a temporary position to supervise the building, it did not remain so for long; almost immediately an agent's house was built adjacent to the Alnwick road and Mr Bertram was installed; he was still there 40 years later when Lord Armstrong's great-nephew and successor was himself raised to the peerage in 1903.

While the Armstrongs took a close personal interest in the developments, it would have been Bertram who handled the day-to-day running of the estate. To judge from their length of service, he was an excellent selector of senior assistant staff. Willie Mavin, the mason, who arrived in 1863 to begin the new house, was still employed at the end of the century. So were William Crosby, the foreman, and Henry Hudson, the head gardener, who arrived respectively in 1864 and 1866. There was, of course, much work to do.

The pleasure grounds around Cragside eventually extended to well over 1,000 acres, with extensions beyond the public roads amounting to a further 700 acres. A double loop of carriage drive about six miles long was contrived around the central hill; and threading the crags, the burns, the valleys and the tops were as many as 40 miles of criss-crossing paths and steps. Drawings, watercolours and early photographs show how much planting was achieved. It is not difficult to believe the oft-quoted remark that seven million shrubs and trees were planted in every available patch of earth and crevice. Nor is it easy to dismiss another tradition, especially as it involves Lady Armstrong, that pennies were exchanged for buckets of earth carried to the rocky upper slopes. No wonder Lord Armstrong could state, apparently without a blush, that 'it had been a pleasure to me to add to the locality's natural beauty by operations which have given healthy employment to a large section of the population'.

The amount of building work in the garden alone was enormous. There were three kinds of rock work. Hundreds of large round boulders were manhandled to create the rock garden between the house and Debdon Burn, which has the appearance of a giant natural scree. Piping from higher up the crag brought water to 'springs', which in turn fed a series of falls and pools. On more level areas, especially to the south of the house, flatter rocks were set into the ground as great pavers giving pleasant access to large intervening areas of planting. But the most dramatic rock work is at the rear of the house, which expanded eastwards almost to touch the face of the quarry from which much of the building stone had been taken. As if to enhance this relation, the quarry face at the south-eastern flank was extended upwards with piles of large rocks laid to ape the natural strata. Plants hanging from the cliff top and wedged into crevices gave a colourful backdrop, especially in the evening sun, to a shelf-like terrace just outside the Drawing Room windows. From here visitors could admire the southern elevation of the house, the pinetum in the valley, and the broad sweep of Upper Coquetdale reaching westwards beyond Rothbury.

Before the trees grew up, these early westward views from the house took in the terraced garden and the open parkland. Not included in that portion of the estate transferred to the National Trust in 1977, they were sold separately later. Purchased by the Trust in 1991, they can once again give visitors a full idea of the range of the Armstrongs' gardening.

Defended by a tall wall from the public road, the terraces were overlooked by both the land steward and the head gardener's houses, and the Clock Tower which regulated the estate. It was here that the more tender plants, vegetables and fruits were nurtured. The glasshouses were once very extensive. On the upper terrace, there was a main conservatory attached to roofed ferneries, and forcing houses with varied humidities. The central terrace had splendid carpet bedding providing a frame for a large orchard house in which fruit trees were tended in pots and mounted on turntables. These allowed ease of access, even growth and a ready supply of soft fruit for the table.

On the lower terrace, a robust cast-iron loggia presided over the curiosity so far north of an Italian garden, with plants defended from the wind by glass walls but without overhead cover. Below this again, a kitchen garden with its back to the roadside wall looked out over undulating parkland sprinkled with specimen trees and clumps. Based on a large glacial deposit, the gentle smoothness of this park as it falls towards the Coquet is in marked and intentional contrast to the wild outline of the crag beyond, where the conifers have outstripped the rocks in making their own jagged edges.

Inevitably, however, where Armstrong was involved, it was the water which gave Cragside its abiding character. Of Armstrong's five major lakes, only Debdon lying west of the Alnwick road remains private and is inaccessible to visitors. It was from there that the original turbine generated electricity to light the house, and in daytime powered a sawmill (see Chapter Three). Tumbleton Lake, formed by damming the Debdon Burn just below the Stables (now the Visitor Centre), provides the head of water to drive the pump which in turn supplies the Basin Tank, a reservoir set high

The glasshouses, conservatories and carpet gardens earlier this century

The Carpet Gardens, Cragside, Rothbury.

above the house. Blackburn Lake, round the hill to the east, was once the largest lake and has a heather thatched boathouse, bearing solid witness to Armstrong's enthusiasm for angling. It now stands high and dry because this lake was probably also the reservoir for the short-lived experimental hydraulic silo at Cragend Farm. At Nelly's Moss at the top of the park are two more lakes, apparently with distinct uses. The lower lake was the main reservoir for the Power House situated 340 feet below, near where Debdon Burn meets the Coquet. It may also have provided an alternative supply for the house. By contrast the Upper Lake could be kept at a more steady level and, with its boathouse, was probably intended for angling or wildfowling.

These lakes are all somewhat remote from the house, and it is Debdon Burn which excites the views from the western windows as it progresses from Tumbleton through a series of pools and little falls, and beneath a variety of bridges. Eventually it tips itself with noise and drama into the gorge where the old mill stood, then to race on past Burnfoot Power House to the Coquet.

At a date probably between 1870 and 1875 Armstrong built the dramatic arched footbridge of steel high over the ravine of the Debdon Burn close to the house. Unique in construction, it has a single central span and two approach spans and is just over 150 feet in length. No certain facts are known about its erection, but doubtless it was made in the Armstrong works at Elswick. It has been restored, but for reasons of safety unfortunately cannot be open to the public. A number of much humbler rustic bridges of wood also connect the various zig-zag paths.

Of the minor buildings on the estate, most of the eight lodges were built at the same time as the original house in 1863–6. So, too, were the Clock

The Stables from across Tumbleton Lake

The Armstrong Cottages in Rothbury

Tower and the nucleus of the garden buildings. The Stables, first built at the same time as the house of 1864, were considerably extended and altered in about 1892–3. Neither the Stables, nor any of the surrounding buildings seem to have been designed by Norman Shaw.

The Armstrong estate was not confined to the great landscape around Cragside. As opportunity arose, Armstrong through gradual purchases built up a landed estate of almost thirty farms, stretching from the rich arable land of the Coquet to the sheep walks of Simonside and the Cheviots. Further afield, the acquisition of Bamburgh Castle included four coastal farms from the old Crewe estate. Nor was property limited to farmland. At Rothbury a terrace of houses called Addycombe Cottages was designed by Norman Shaw in the early 1870s. Armstrong was able to provide building land for churches in both Thropton and Rothbury. Among other charitable works there was one which linked Armstrong's earliest days in Rothbury with his declining years. He recorded that his first memory

of Rothbury was staying in a house which belonged to the family friends, the Donkins. This would have been about 1820; over seventy years later Armstrong, by then owner of derelict houses on the site (which may have been a bequest from Armorer Donkin), agreed to give the land for a new Congregational church. And, because one of the old houses had served as a rather primitive almshouse, he erected the Armstrong Cottages at the east end of Rothbury in memory of his mother. As William Weaver Tomlinson wrote in *The Comprehensive Guide to the County of Northumberland* in 1888:

Words are inadequate to describe the wonderful transformation which Lord Armstrong has made on the barren hill-side as it existed previous to 1863. Every natural advantage has been utilized by the great magician. Shrubs and trees that grow best in exposed situations have been planted among the boulders of Cragside with admirable results. Rhododendrons, azaleas, and other plants of rich coloured bloom, with native heather, bracken and ling, soften and brighten the hard features of the landscape till it smiles again.

BIBLIOGRAPHY

ASLET, Clive, 'Cragside, Northumberland', *Country Life*, clxviii, 4 September 1980, p. 759.

BOWERS, B., *A History of Electric Light and Power*, Peter Peregrinus in association with Science Museum, London, 1982.

DIBDIN, E. Rimbault, 'Lord Armstrong's Collection of Modern Pictures', *Magazine of Art*, xiv, 1891, pp. 158–65, 193–9.

DIXON, David Dippie, *Upper Coquetdale*, 1903 [reprinted 1974], pp. 430–42.

DOUGAN, David, *The Great Gunmaker*, Frank Graham, Newcastle, 1970.

GIROUARD, Mark, 'Cragside – I and II', *Country Life*, cxlvi, 18, 25 December 1969, pp. 1640, 1694; *The Victorian Country House*, 1971, pp. 141–6.

IRLAM, Geoffrey A., *Domestic Engineering at Cragside; Electricity Supply at Cragside*, Association of Industrial Archaeology in association with the National Trust, 1991.

LINSLEY, Stafford, 'William George Armstrong, 1st Lord Armstrong of Cragside', *Dictionary of Business Biography*, 1984–6.

McKENZIE, Peter, *The Life and Times of Sir William George Armstrong of Cragside*, Longhirst, Newcastle, 1983.

MACLEOD, Dianne Sachko, 'Mid-Victorian patronage of the arts: F. G. Stephens's "The Private Collections of England"', *Burlington Magazine*, cxxviii, August 1986, pp. 597–607; 'Art collecting and Victorian middle-class taste', *Art History*, x, September 1987, pp. 328–50; 'Private and public patronage in Victorian Newcastle', *Journal of the Warburg and Courtauld Institutes*, lii, 1989, pp. 188–208.

PETTIT, Sheila, 'Hunt the Wallpaper', *National Trust Magazine*, No. 33, Spring 1980.

PUGH, B., *The Hydraulic Age*, Mechanical Engineering Publications 1980.

RENNISON, R. W., *Water to Tyneside – A History of the Newcastle and Gateshead Water Company*, Newcastle and Gateshead Water Company, Newcastle, 1979.

SAINT, Andrew, *Richard Norman Shaw*, 1976.

STEPHENS, F. G., 'Galleries near Newcastle', *Athenaeum*, 13 September 1873, pp. 342–4.

TAYLOR, Robert S., 'Swan's Electric Light at Cragside', *National Trust Studies*, 1980.

TYNE AND WEAR MUSEUMS SERVICE, *Pre-Raphaelites: Painters and Patrons in the North East*, Newcastle, 1989.

Old articles in *Building News*, 10 May 1872; *The World*, 29 January 1879; *The Gardener's Chronicle*, 11 September 1880; *The Engineer*, 21 January 1881; *The Electrician*, vi, 1880–1, p. 153; *The Graphic*, 2 April 1881; *The British Architect*, 20, 27 May 1881; *Newcastle Daily Journal*, supplements for Royal Visit to Cragside, 1884; *The Monthly Chronicle of North Country Lore and Legend*, October 1887, January 1889 and August 1891; *Ludgate Monthly*, v, 1893, pp. 571–82; *Cassier's Magazine*, ix, 1895–6, pp. 488–94; *Country Life*, 14 April 1900; *Newcastle Journal*, 28 December 1900; *The Northern Counties Magazine*, i, 1900–1, pp. 324–9; *The Throne*, 4 August 1906.

There are drawings for Cragside in the Norman Shaw collections at the Royal Institute of British Architects and the Royal Academy in London. Samples of some of the early wallpapers remain among the ledgers of Cowtan, now deposited at the Victoria and Albert Museum. Christie's catalogues for 20 and 24 June 1910 list the paintings and blue-and-white china sold at that date.

INDEX